The Irony of Irish Democracy

The Irony of Irish Democracy

The Impact of Political Culture on Administrative and Democratic Political Development in Ireland

David E. Schmitt
Northeastern University

Lexington Books
D. C. Heath and Company
Lexington, Massachusetts
Toronto   London

Library of Congress Cataloging in Publication Data

Schmitt, David E.
    The irony of Irish democracy.

    Bibliography: p. 97
    1. Ireland—Politics and government—1922—
    2. Ireland—Social conditions.
I. Title.
DA963.S35 1973   301.5'92'09415   73-8646
ISBN 0-669-86769-1

Copyright ©1973 by D. C. Heath and Company

Published simultaneously in Canada.

Printed in the United States of America.

International Standard Book Number: 0-669-86769-1

Library of Congress Catalog Card Number: 73-8646

For Gabrielle

Contents

Acknowledgments

The writer wishes to acknowledge the kind assistance of the library personnel of Trinity College, Dublin, the National Library of Ireland, the Institute of Public Administration (Dublin), the Economic and Social Research Institute (Dublin), and the Linenhall Library (Belfast). The able assistance of Paula Howard of the Linenhall Library, Mary Prendergast of the Institute of Public Administration library, and Maureen Doran-O'Reilly of the Economic and Social Research Institute is especially appreciated.

Discussions with the following scholars were of particular help: Basil Chubb of Trinity College; Brian Farrell and Thomas Garvin of University College, Dublin; Patrick Quinlan of University College, Cork; John Whyte of Queen's University, Belfast; John Raven, Ian Hart, and C. T. Whelan of the Economic and Social Research Institute; Desmond Roche and Frank Litton of the Institute of Public Administration; M. Donald Hancock, Carl Leiden, William S. Livingston and Emmette S. Redford of the University of Texas at Austin; and David Barkley, George Berkley, James Medeiros, and my other colleagues at Northeastern University. Although politicians, administrators, and interest-group leaders were assured of anonymity their comments were of great benefit.

The late Patrick M. Condron, as well as Professor Patrick Quinlan and Maoilseachlainn O Caollai were particularly helpful in their generous assistance and advice. Brian Farrell and John Whyte read the manuscript and made valuable suggestions; they were also most helpful in pointing out source material. Frank Munger of the University of North Carolina, Ian Hart, Francis Litton, Stein Larsen of the University of Bergen, Norway, John Raven, and C. T. Whelan generously consented to my utilization of their unpublished material. During my undergraduate years at Miami University (Ohio), I was particularly inspired by the teaching of Reo M. Christenson and Joseph Black (now of the Rockefeller Foundation). My greatest intellectual debt is to Professor William S. Livingston of the University of Texas, whose detailed suggestions, guidance, and continuing support have been of great benefit to this study, and to my scholarly development.

The assistance of Mr. and Mrs. Jeremiah Lynch, Mr. and Mrs. John G. Hewitt, Mr. and Mrs. Frank Loughran, the late Mr. Malachy J. Kealy and his family, Mrs. Catherin McLoughlin, Mrs. Margaret O'Sullivan, Mr. and Mrs. Peter Toolin, the Condron family of Tevenie, Dromina, as well as Mr. and Mrs. Robert G. Backus, Mrs. Janet Life, my mother Mrs. Violet Schmitt, and Miss Virginia Vicars was of invaluable help. The cooperation and support of Professors R. Gregg Wilfong and Walter Jones, as well as Deans Arthur Fitzgerald, Robert Shepard, and Sidney Herman, all of Northeastern University, aided the completion of this project. The gracious and skilled typing assistance by Mrs. Marilyn Zazlaw and Mrs. Kedron Oberndorf was of great help.

Naturally the greatest burden of the study fell upon my wife, Gabrielle, and the children, Alana and Michael. Their sacrifices are greatly appreciated. Above all, the abiding support of Gabrielle, to whom this book is dedicated, proved a major source of inspiration. Her understanding, good humor, and steadfastness assisted more than anything else the successful completion of this book.

Errors, limitations, and the specific viewpoint of this study are, of course, my personal responsibility.

The Irony of Irish Democracy

1 Introduction

One of the major developments in the field of comparative government since World War II has been the shift in emphasis from the Western political systems of North America, Europe, and the "white" Commonwealth nations to the newly emergent nations in Asia and Africa, as well as to the political systems of Latin America. This shift was generated by the greatly increased visibility and importance of these systems during their struggles for independence and by their failure to establish effective, stable, democratic structures and processes.[1]

An important consequence of the emphasis upon Third-World politics has been a proliferation of literature about the problems and processes of political development.[2] As used herein the term "political development" refers to the processes by which political systems institutionalize new patterns of organizations and procedures for confronting political and administrative needs, and for dealing with rising demands, increasing groups and new goals brought on by economic and social modernization.[3] Democratic political development is that variety of political development characterized by relatively honest elections, free speech, freedom of assembly, a free press, and the opportunity for open competition for control of government.

Because the Republic of Ireland was a colonized land and won its independence only in the twentieth century, and because it has been seldom studied from an explicitly developmental framework, an analysis of its political development in light of contemporary concepts and approaches can be quite useful. Moreover, since Ireland gained independence only in the 1920s it may hold particular interest to students of Third-World politics interested in the processes by which new nations develop politically.

The present study will be particularly concerned with the role of political culture in Ireland in the process of democratic political development since independence. Lucian Pye and Sidney Verba define political culture as ". . . the system of empirical beliefs, expressive symbols, and values which defines the situation in which political action takes place."[4] Thus, any politically relevant beliefs and values are included in the definition even if they are social in nature. The present study, for instance, will be particularly concerned with authoritarianism and personalism in social relations—two especially pronounced and important features of Irish political culture.

The political cultures of new nations frequently are a great impediment

1

to political development. In one of the most important studies in the literature, Lucian Pye observed that "the real problem in political development is . . . the extent to which the socialization process of a people provides them with the necessary associational sentiments so that they can have considerable conflict without destroying the stability of the system."[5] He notes that cultural dimensions essential to favorable associational norms, such as interpersonal trust, are determined by basic cultural aspects of society—child-rearing practices, for instance. Examples include the inconsistent reactions by Burmese mothers to their children and the Burmese practice of teaching children to distrust those outside the family, which contributes to feelings of political distrust.[6]

Political cultures have a significant role in the process of institutionalization or ". . . the process by which organizations and procedures acquire value and stability."[7] As Geertz stated, for example, cultural fragmentation among ethnic and religious groups can lead to a number of problems, including civil war.[8] Indeed, Enloe has noted that the conflict in Northern Ireland can be viewed in terms of cultural or ethnic conflict.[9] Moreover, because all modern governments need a substantial degree of public support in order to survive and develop politically, the role of culture in furthering or impeding a sense of national identity and loyalty is a matter of great concern to students of developmental politics. Finally, the ability of citizens to cooperate greatly affects the capacity of the political system to create viable organizations.

These issues will constitute the major emphasis of the present undertaking. Consideration of the role of political culture in the creation of national loyalties and consideration of the role of culture in determining the establishment of effective organizations and democratic political institutions will be of particular concern. As noted, emphasis will be placed on two features of Irish political culture that are significant for political development in general, and democratic political development in particular, namely, the degree of authoritarianism and personalism in the Irish political system.[10]

The personalistic dimensions of the Irish political culture will be analyzed in terms of their implications for the development of viable organizations and political processes. Attention will be given to the effect of personalism on organizational cohesiveness, adaptability, and efficiency. Particular issues to be considered with respect to these administrative ideals include administrative legitimacy, organizational communication, and administrative corruption.

Authoritarianism will be dealt with in a somewhat different manner. A frequent feature of the literature on political culture is the argument that habitual deference to authority helps maintain and stabilize developing political systems. Robert Ward and others have noted that traditional values can facilitate political development in authoritarian regimes and therefore help provide for the later development of democratic political processes.[11] The present study, however, will investigate the proposition that authoritarian norms can also help support democratic institutions and that these democratic institutions, as well as economic modernization, may help in the eventual establishment of democratic political norms. The analysis of authoritarianism in Ireland will be concerned also with the consequences of deferential values for the development of viable organizations. It will be argued that, ironically, authoritarian and personalistic norms have facilitated democratic political development in Ireland and, further, that they have facilitated the establishment of effective organizations.

It is hoped that this book will contribute to the understanding of Irish political development and, perhaps, contribute to the ongoing debate on Irish administrative and political reform. Additionally, this work provides a case study that may have meaning and utility for students of the developing areas, as well as for those interested in modern political systems. For, even though modern nations are presumably well developed in terms of organizational and political complexity, their capacity to deal with increasing demands is now threatened, especially by the decline in popular support among important social sectors such as young people. Since part of this problem results from the depersonalizing aspects of modern bureaucracy, the implications of Irish personalism for the modern systems may be of considerable importance. No nation is ever completely developed, and all nations may experience institutional or political decay.

For readers unfamiliar with Ireland, the second chapter provides a brief discussion of the operation and structures of the Irish political system. Similarly, chapter three covers some ground familiar to Irish readers but does deal with newer concepts such as social mobilization. Since cultural change has been so pronounced since the end of World War II and especially since the 1950s, chapter six will deal with some of these changes under the general heading of secularization. Moreover, because the very existence of the Republic has such an important bearing upon the politics of Northern Ireland, implications of these changes for political development in the troubled North will be briefly considered as will the impact of Northern politics on the Republic.

The research for the present study was conducted in Ireland during 1967, 1969-1970, and the spring of 1973. It included discussions with politicians (including Cabinet members, TD's and Senators), administrators at various levels, interest-group leaders, scholars, journalists, and people in all walks of life. Naturally, library materials such as books, articles, and government documents were of basic use as were several published and unpublished survey projects. Participant observation was also quite helpful since the author has interacted with people in typical day-to-day activities involving various facets of social and political life. Although visiting and living with several families in various parts of Ireland helped provide many insights and some of the opportunities for direct interaction, later specific descriptions of Irish society and family life do not necessarily describe these particular gracious and hospitable people. For the most part, interview sources have been kept confidential in order to honor the guarantee (and frequent requests) for anonymity.

2

The Irish Social and Political Systems

The principal goal of the present chapter is to provide a background for the analysis that follows in later chapters. Mention of Irish geography, for example, will help explain Ireland's comparative isolation from European culture as well as its absorption of many aspects of the British political culture. Similarly, discussion of the democratic character of the Irish political system will illustrate the significance of Ireland as a case study for students of democratic political development and provide a background for the next chapter, which analyzes the processes by which democracy was achieved in Ireland.

The Physical, Economic, and Social Settings

Ireland is an island Republic separated from continental Europe not only by water, but also by Britain. Indeed, its proximity to England has been a crucial factor for its historical development. Moreover, the entire island is quite small; its total area is 32,595 square miles, of which 27,136 square miles comprises the Republic, which, thus, has a slightly larger land mass than the state of West Virginia.

The Republic, therefore, dominates the land mass of the island. Northern Ireland, a part of the United Kingdom, consists of merely six counties of northeastern Ireland. Until 1972, its million and a half people existed under a Protestant-dominated government favoring retention of the link with Britain; since March 1972, the United Kingdom government has exercised direct rule. Although this book concerns the Republic, and not Northern Ireland, the two political systems have an effect upon one another. Hence, a later chapter will deal with the reciprocal influence between North and South.

The population of the Republic is only 2,978,248, a fact that has important implications for the political style of the country. Although the trend toward urbanization has been under way since the last century, nearly half the population still lives in rural areas. Moreover, Dublin, with a population of 567,866, is a true capital city, playing the dominant role in the political, economic, and social life of Irish society.[1]

The Irish Republic is predominantly Roman Catholic; about ninety-five percent of the population as of 1961 belonged to the Roman Catholic church.[2]

5

Moreover, unlike some nations having a high statistical percentage of Roman Catholics, most Irishmen take their religion quite seriously. Most people attend church services regularly. Indeed, among Catholics the weekly attendance at mass is about ninety-five percent.[3] References to the Church and to religion are common in both private and public speech.

The Economy

Economically, Ireland has made great strides in the past fifteen years, and the country is in a state of economic transition. To a considerable extent, this can be attributed to greater Government concern with economic planning. Indeed, following the Government's implementation of a five-year program for economic development after 1958, developmental planning became a matter of principal concern for a variety of public and private agencies. The growing literature on this subject and the continuing emphasis upon economic development by the Irish government suggests, in fact, a shift from the earlier laissez faire attitude to one of intensive state planning.[4]

Despite economic advances in recent years, however, Ireland remains one of the poorest nations in Western Europe. The country had a per-capita gross national product of $1,292 in 1970; only Spain and Portugal had lower per-capita incomes.[5] Furthermore, the per-capita income figure overlooks the distribution of wealth. In the West of Ireland, where land is often poor and the density of population high, compared with other sections of rural Ireland, incomes by American standards remain at the poverty level. Moreover, economic development in Ireland has fallen behind government expectations; labor unrest has increased in recent years and important strikes have occurred in key industries, such as banking and transport. Inflation in Ireland in 1972 was the highest of the EEC nations. The economic problem is compounded, moreover, by the paucity of natural resources. To be sure, new mineral deposits have led to a growing industry in mining of metals, but the deposits are not sufficient for a radical improvement of the Irish economy. The economy remains significantly rural. Agriculture produce accounts for more than half of the nation's exports, and about thirty-one percent of Ireland's work force is engaged in agricultural occupations.[6]

Despite its political independence, Ireland's economy is closely tied to that of Great Britain. Although Ireland has its own currency, it is pegged to the value of the British pound, and British currency is accepted and used throughout the Republic. The United Kingdom purchases approximately seventy percent of all Irish exports, and accounts for fifty-one percent of Irish imports.[7] This pattern of reciprocal trade, moreover, has been formalized by agreements between Ireland and the United Kingdom which provide for guaranteed prices for Irish commodities in return for Irish purchases of

British products. Although the point is often exaggerated by Irish radical nationalist organizations, such as the Sinn Féin parties, decisions by the British government have constrained the range of options available to Irish political leaders in economic matters.

Of course, entry into the Common Market will alter Ireland's economic and political relations with Britain and will provide a new potential for economic growth; but without significant natural resources it is unlikely that Ireland will become a rich nation in the foreseeable future. Moreover, the argument is still made by ardent nationalists that Ireland's cultural and political autonomy will be further submerged in the even larger political and economic grouping of the EEC.

The Irish Political System

By almost any criteria the Republic of Ireland ranks as one of the most stable and effective political democracies. Since independence there has never been a successful coup d'etat, and elections have been free and open. Moreover, although censorship is greater in Ireland than in most democratic nations, this censorship rarely extends to the basic political freedoms. Thus, while films must be approved by a censorship board, and while books and magazines can be banned on issues of morality, political materials and speeches are not normally subject to the same kinds of restraint.[8] Although one party, Fianna Fáil, has been dominant in Irish politics for most of the period since 1932, Ireland is by no means a rigid one-party state. Indeed, a National Coalition of Fine Gael and Labour party politicians now comprise the Government, and they appear to have won the 1973 national elections, in large part on the basis of their party program. There is genuine opportunity for alternation of parties in power.

The Cabinet

The structure of Irish government, for the most part, follows the British model. The Cabinet is usually composed of leaders of the majority party in the Dáil (lower house) or, in the case of a coalition government, the leaders of the parties forming the coalition. The Irish Cabinet, however, is a more formal institution than its British counterpart, and the constitution explicitly gives it executive power and charges it with the collective responsibility for the departments of state and for the preparation of the annual budget.[9] "The Cabinet still holds within itself a near-monopoly of major public decisions. . . ."[10]

The Taoiseach (Prime Minister), who is normally leader of his party, heads the Cabinet and usually has a predominant role in it.[11] Although he must take cognizance of major factions and leaders within his party in the selection of his Cabinet, he has a relatively free hand in choosing members of the Government and in assigning departmental responsibilities. Moreover, through the Department of the Taoiseach, he has the task of coordinating the efforts of the various departments. It is the Taoiseach, for example, who determines the agenda of Cabinet meetings, decides when to convene and dissolve the Dáil, and acts as spokesman for the Government.[12]

Yet the power of the Taoiseach depends upon factors other than formal constitutional powers and structural arrangements. The strong leadership of Eamon de Valera, because of his dominant personality and a united party, gave the position of Taoiseach predominance in the Cabinet. Not only did he regularly impose his policy decisions on the Government, but also he could, if necessary, operate in a personalistic manner within the Cabinet, bypassing normal procedures. On the other hand, Costello, as head of his first interparty Government, was much more limited in his ability to make decisions on his own because his Cabinet was composed of members of different parties with diverse viewpoints concerning matters of policy. In short, although the constitution gives the Taoiseach the legal basis for leading the Government, much depends on his personality, the popular support he enjoys, and the degree of the party unity within his Cabinet and within the Dáil.[13]

Yet the Cabinet as a whole retains more policy making powers than does its counterpart in Great Britain. Ireland is a small nation with a comparatively simple administrative structure, and its Government has a smaller administrative load. Unlike the British Cabinet, the Irish Cabinet has no extensive system of committees to deal with particular problem areas. To be sure, committees were set up during the interparty Governments (1948-51 and 1954-57), but did not perform key functions. The role of committees in the new coalition Government is not yet clear; however, the smaller work load will enable the Irish Cabinet to operate with fewer committees than its British counterpart. Yet, as the later mention of internal Cabinet conflict over the Republic's role in the Northern Irish crisis makes clear, neither Cabinet cohesiveness nor Teaoiseach supervision is assured. Nevertheless, the Cabinet is the dominant body in Irish politics.[14]

Parliament

The Oireachtas (the bicameral Parliament) does not play a central role in the Irish political system.[15] The membership of both houses is small—the Dáil has 144 Deputies and the Senate has 60 Senators—and hence there is little need for a complex committee system, all the more so since the tasks of governing in Ireland are less complex. Indeed, the Irish Dáil, which is the dominant house, has an even less significant committee system than does the British Parliament. The major Dáil committee is the Public Accounts Committee, which has the job of inspecting the public audit prepared by the comptroller and the auditor general, but this is a relatively minor responsibility. The committee thus plays a relatively small role except, perhaps, in unusual circumstances such as the crisis generated by the Northern conflict. Most significant committee work is in fact carried out by committees of the whole house.[16] Also, the Dáil has little part in the initiation of legislation. With a system of responsible party government, and with the Taoiseach and the Cabinet determining which matters will be considered by the house, the Government usually is assured of Dáil approval of its programs. The opposition party can, of course, oppose Government measures through parliamentary debate and by informal means. It can even attempt to win public support for its position. But, under normal circumstances, the Dáil lacks the numerical strength to block the Government's policy measures.

The rules for debate, and for the introduction and passage of bills are also similar to those of the British Parliament. Dáil proceedings are directed by a chairman (Ceann Comhairle), whose task it is to serve as an impartial speaker of the house. His role, in other words, is to maintain order, to conduct the debate, and to ensure that all sides receive a fair hearing. The opposition, however, is not in a position to impede seriously the progress of legislation under consideration by the Dáil because of the Government's recourse to closure. In sum, because of party loyalty and ultimate Government control of the introduction and passage of legislation, opposition parties can, at best, hope to win support for their position through publicity generated by parliamentary debate.[17]

Furthermore, parliamentary questions do not usually constitute a serious check on government activities. Most questions, for example, are concerned with purely local matters of routine nature. Questions are frequently asked merely to demonstrate to local constituents that the deputy is interested in their problems. Moreover, because the Government has much better access to information, it is often difficult for those outside the Cabinet to make accurate assessments of the Government's responses. Nevertheless, the opportunity to question members of the Government serves as a deterrent to arbitrary Government action. Additionally, because question time is given serious attention by the news media, it, as well, serves as a means of placing opposition views before the public.[18]

Another reason for the Dáil's limited role in the legislative process has been its lack of facilities. Deputies have had little secretarial help and inadequate funds for staff assistance, though assistance has increased somewhat in recent years. Moreover, deputies see their primary role as one of assisting local constituents in their dealings with the government bureaucracy; indeed, most of their time, when not in Dáil sessions, is spent doing favors for constituents.[19]

The Irish Senate has an even smaller role than the Dáil in the legislative process. Its principal power is its capacity to delay passage of government legislation, but that capacity is even more limited than that of the British House of Lords. With respect to money bills, the Senate has 21 days to review any legislation passed by the Dáil. If it has not acted within that period, the bill becomes law. With respect to other bills, the maximum period of consideration allowed the Senate is 90 days, although the bill cannot become law for a period of 180 days if the Senate rejects it. Again, the Dáil may or may not accept the Senate's recommendations and is free to override a Senate rejection. Indeed, there is even a procedure designed to meet emergencies, whereby the maximum time for consideration for a bill can be reduced by a resolution of the Dáil when approved by the president.[20]

Although the constitution provides that as many as two senators may be members of the Cabinet, since 1938 only one senator has, in fact, been given a Cabinet appointment, and in that instance it was because he had lost the election for a seat in the Dáil.[21] The Senate usually meets for less than 30 days each year.

Nonetheless, the Senate does serve some useful purposes. The quality of debate is often high, and senatorial proceedings receive at least some consideration by the press even if substantially less than the Dáil. Also, the Senate sometimes makes useful changes in bills adopted by the lower house. The Senate Select Committee on Statutory Instruments serves, at least, as a partial check on the increasing number of policy decisions made by the Irish bureaucracy. Yet, this committee's principal task is to ensure that government departments and state-sponsored bodies comply with formal legal criteria, such as the requirement that statutory instruments be published. Further, the Select Committee on Statutory Instruments has power to report its conclusions only to the Senate. It does not deal with all aspects of administrative law and cannot deal with matters of policy.[22]

The constitution provides that a majority of the Senate, and at least one-third of the Dáil, can request that the president decline to sign a bill on the ground that the bill is of such national significance that it ought to be submitted to the public by means of a referendum. The president, however, has discretionary power and can either accept or reject the recommendation after consultation with a body called the Council of State; this is an infrequently utilized advisory body which consists of high past and present public officials such as the taoiseach, chief justice, attorney general, and past presidents and chief justices, as well as members appointed by the president.[23]

About the only other function senators have is one shared with deputies, namely to serve as ombudsmen, when called upon on behalf of citizens to intercede in the administrative processes of the state. On balance one must conclude that the Senate has a marginal role in the Irish political system.

The President

Similarly, the president of Ireland has a relatively minor role, although he possesses some formal powers that give him greater significance than that of mere figurehead. Yet, even as a ceremonial figurehead, the role of an Irish president may have real symbolic importance. To be sure, secular heads-of-state in democratic political systems do not have the same legitimizing significance as constitutional monarchs who are popular with their citizens. Nevertheless, when occupied by a man like de Valera the presidency has a popular appeal that transcends considerations of formal powers. A principal hero of the struggle for independence from Britain, a leader of the Republican faction during the Civil War, leader of the Fianna Fáil party and the past Taoiseach, the aged de Valera undoubtedly instilled in the office a dignity and emotional appeal not often found surrounding presidents.

In addition, the office has formal powers designed to make the Irish president a defender of the constitution. Elected for a seven-year term by direct vote, the president performs the usual functions of any head-of-state in a parliamentary system. He appoints the Taoiseach on the advice of the Dáil, and he appoints the members of the Government on the advice of the Taoiseach and the Dáil. And, again, on the advice of the Taoiseach, the president summons and dissolves the Dáil. He may, however, refuse to accept the Taoiseach's recommendation to dissolve the Dáil, even if a Taoiseach no longer retains the support of a majority of the Dáil. Although the president has never refused to grant a dissolution, it is possible that in a time of great political instability he might do so, and thus help in the achievement of peaceful political compromises. But such a refusal would raise some very serious constitutional questions which, never having been faced, have never been resolved.

After seeking the advice of the Council of State, the president may refer a bill to the Supreme Court to determine whether it is "repugnant" to the constitution. As noted earlier, the president may initiate a referendum on a bill stated to be of great national importance by a majority of the Senate and at least one-third of the Dáil. Furthermore, after consulting the Council of State, he may at any time summon a meeting of either house. Thus, although seldom used, these formal powers give the Irish president a position of great potential significance, but one of little practical influence in the operation of the political system. Under normal circumstances, his role is primarily ceremonial and symbolic.[24]

The Electoral System

Election to the Dáil is by means of preferential voting, with quota counting. The number of seats in each district varies between three and five, and there is an average of about 20,000 constituents for each deputy, a much lower ratio than exists in the United States or Britain. The constitution does not set an upper limit on the number of seats per district, but sets a lower limit of three. The Government is in a position to determine the upper limit to the number of deputies per district because it is normally assured of a majority of votes in the Dáil. Lower numbers of seats per district are preferred by the major parties, since this gives less advantage to the smaller parties. Nevertheless, and particularly in the five-member districts (of which only two remain), the system does appear to assist smaller parties.[25]

Under the Irish system of proportional representation the voter indicates his order of preference for the candidates in his district, and by means of a quota system, those candidates achieving the quota are declared elected. Then the surplus votes of the candidate declared elected are transferred to other candidates on the basis of the order of preferences listed on the ballots. This process continues as additional candidates are declared elected until all seats in the constituency have been filled. If insufficient surplus votes from winners are available the candidate with the fewest votes is eliminated, and his votes are then redistributed according to the next preference on the ballot.[26]

Election to the Senate is based partly on indirect nomination and partly on corporate representation. Thus, the Irish Senate represents an interesting attempt at functional representation. To help guarantee a Government majority in the upper house, eleven of the Senate's sixty members are nominated directly by the Taoiseach. To provide representation for the educational sector, six senators are elected mainly by Irish citizens who hold degrees. More precisely, three senators are elected by those citizens having a degree from the National University (a predominantly Catholic public university), and three are elected by eligible citizens holding degrees or scholarships from the University of Dublin (Trinity College), which is predominantly Protestant.

The other forty-three members of the Senate are elected by members of the Dáil, the Senate itself, and the councils of counties and county boroughs in a system of proportional representation, using the single transferable vote. The functional aspect of the election of these forty-three senators derives from the fact that candidates are elected from five panels, representing major interests in the society as follows: (1) language and culture, literature, art, and other professional interests; (2) agriculture and fishing; (3) labor; (4) industry and commerce; and (5) public administration and social services. There are two nominating bodies for each of the five panels. One consists of four members of the Houses of the Oireachtas, and the other consists of registered nominating bodies made up, essentially, of various groups included under the heading of one of the above classifications. Thus, each panel comprises two sub-panels, one containing the nominees of the members of the Houses of Oireachtas and the other consisting of nominees of interest organizations.[27]

The interesting point about this attempt at functional representation, however, is that the realities of the party system make it impossible for functional representation to work in practice. In other words, rather than being organized on the basis of functional divisions, the Senate, in practice, is organized on a party basis. The reason for this is that most of the senators elected from the five panels have, typically, been those nominated by politicians of the Oireachtas, and most of the electors are themselves party politicians.[28]

The electoral processes have important implications for the style of politics. First, with a small number of constituents, opportunities for face-to-face interaction between constituents and deputies, and for personal consideration by the deputies of constituents' problems are greatly increased. Furthermore, although representatives may face heavy competition in other kinds of electoral systems, in a multimember district with elections based on preferential voting, candidates and elected deputies are forced into a particularly competitive role. Even members of the same party may be in competition with one another for the support of the voters. Thus, the electoral system places great additional pressures on members of the lower house to compete for votes through such means as doing favors for constituents.[29] The method of electing senators places less pressure on them to run errands for constituents, although interestingly, senators, too, are expected by Irish citizens to intercede for them in the administrative process.

Parties

With respect to political parties, Ireland today has a three-party system with one stable majority party (Fianna Fáil), one stable "majority-bent" party (Fine Gael), and one small, stable minority party.[30] But though Fianna Fail is clearly the largest party, it has often won less than a majority of the seats in the Dáil, and thus has had to rely upon the support of minor parties and independent deputies. Since 1932 there have been three interparty Governments composed of Fine Gael, which is the principal opposition party, Labour, and other minor parties. As noted earlier, it is the National Coalition of Labour and Fine Gael that now holds office. Thus, to reiterate, despite the former dominant role of Fianna Fáil in the politics of the Irish Republic, there exists genuine opportunity for the alternation of governments.

The Labour Party is the principal minor party; and although it had drawn most of its support from the eastern and southern regions of the nation, it now has increasing support in urban areas. Lacking a strong basis for nationwide support it cannot, by itself, form a Government, but it is presently a member of the coalition Cabinet. It is, also, less conservative than either Fianna Fáil or Fine Gael, and is therefore an important source of innovation because its policy proposals can stimulate the major parties to move to the left of their own programs.[31] Small minor parties and independent members of the Dáil, though not in themselves of great significance, have provided a basis for the formation of interparty coalition Governments.

Since Duverger wrote *Political Parties* there has been considerable disagreement regarding the effect of electoral systems upon party systems, although most political scientists would probably agree that Duverger originally overstated the significance of that influence.[32] Even though Irish experience supports the argument that electoral systems help shape party systems, it also supports the argument that other considerations, such as social and cultural divisions and historical factors, are of still greater consequence. As will be shown in the following chapter, for example, Fianna Fáil and Fine Gael originally emerged as the parties representing the pro-Treaty and anti-Treaty forces, and they have maintained their support largely on the basis of those positions during the struggle over the Treaty issue.

Yet the existence of a proportional representation system undoubtedly facilitated the survival of the smaller parties and independents, for in a single-member constituency system they would be seriously handicapped unless they could establish significant strength on a regional basis. On the other hand, small-member constituencies impeded the development of even stronger minor parties.

The Public Bureaucracy

The government bureaucracy in Ireland facilitated the development of an effective, democratic policy. In most democratic societies, however, the growing tasks of government have so greatly increased the load on the public sector that public-policy decisions, increasingly, are made by the administrative branch. Despite the relatively small size of Ireland, administrative decisions have, as well, become a major source of public policy in the Irish Republic.

It should be made clear at the outset that, later discussions of personalism in the administrative process notwithstanding, the Irish undoubtedly have one of the most honest administrations to be found anywhere. Indeed, political behavior is relatively honest throughout the political system, and spoils are of limited importance. Moreover, although many senior Irish administrators have received only secondary-school training, they are nevertheless professionals, and like the British administrators are for the most part generalists rather than specialists. There is little interdepartmental mobility, however, so administrators sometimes acquire a strongly departmental viewpoint. In sum, the overall structure of the Irish civil service is very similar to the British.

Without going into an extended discussion of the various government departments, it will be merely mentioned that Ireland possesses a rather typical division of departmental functions—having such departments as External Affairs, Finance (which has a control function similar to its counterpart in Britain), Defence, and Social Welfare. One of the most unusual departments, however, is the Department of the Gaeltacht, which has responsibility for the affairs of the Irish-speaking areas. Although the Irish-language-revival movement is now weaker than it was early in this century, efforts to preserve the native language still receive support in Ireland by such means as requiring that the language be taught in the national schools, requiring that government documents be published in both English and Irish, and by means of a number of special activities. The discussion of the Department of the Gaeltacht and the language movement is important because it illustrates the nationalist dimension of the Irish political culture.[33]

One important consequence of Ireland's comparatively low level of economic development is that, despite a philosophical preference for private enterprise, political leaders have been forced to intervene not only to provide basic capital services such as power and roads, but also to promote industry. In fact, except for a capitalistic bias and a preference for the profit motive even in public enterprises, one can conclude that the economy of Ireland is heavily socialized. This means, of course, that the government needs a larger administrative branch to handle its economic activities.

The principal means of achieving economic development, especially in recent years, has been through semiautonomous, state-sponsored bodies rather than through the creation of new departments or the expansion of old ones. According to a study conducted by Garret FitzGerald, state-sponsored bodies by 1963 had accounted for over thirty-five percent of personnel employed by the state.[34] One of the most significant points concerning state-sponsored bodies for present purposes, however, is that unlike the Irish civil service as a whole, there is some evidence that appointments, especially to governing boards, are made on the basis of party connections rather than on the basis of professional competency.[35] Nevertheless, these appointments are a minor part of the total picture, and on balance it is quite clear that Irish public employees, despite limitations to be noted later, are honest professionals who may be compared favorably with administrators in other democratic political systems.

Local Government

A final aspect of public administration in Ireland is local government. Though it is often neglected by both citizens and analysts, in human terms some of the most important political questions—and thus the allocation of some of the most valuable political benefits—are often decided on the local level. More significant for present purposes is the point that an acquaintance with the Irish system of local government will provide insight into the political norms of the Irish public and the Irish leaders, as well as information on the distribution of power within the Irish political system.

Despite attempts under the Union with Great Britain to initiate programs of local self-government, the system of local government as it exists today is dominated almost exclusively by the central government administration, especially the Department of Local Government. The organization of local government resembles a council-manager system. Yet the councils do not select managers nor can they easily fire them. It is not surprising that centralized personnel and budgetary controls enable Dublin and the managers to dominate local administration. Even in the United States, where councils often have more direct controls over managers, the managers in practice have the expertise, information, and time to develop a predominant role.

Yet the local councillors have an important political role because they act as intermediaries between citizens and bureaucrats. Normally councillors are residents of the area they serve, and they add a personal touch to the processes of government. But, by concentrating on their role as messengers for local citizens, they weaken still further their capacity to deal with policy issues. Moreover, the Irish public is not greatly troubled by the minor policymaking role of councillors. As demonstrated by Francis Litton's as yet unpublished survey of Dubliners, the Dublin electorate was not greatly disturbed when the central government suspended the Dublin City Council in 1969 in a dispute over tax rates.[36] In any event, Ireland is undergoing administrative reform, and there is a continuing dialogue on the possible types of reform of local government.[37]

Interest Groups

Like other Western democracies, Ireland has a highly developed system of organized interest groups representing most sectors of Irish society. It may be useful to describe briefly some of the major ones. Although the Irish labor movement has often been criticized for its lack of unity, its importance in recent years is indicated by the many union-sponsored strikes which have impeded economic growth. Despite the large number of trade unions, several organizations such as the Irish Transport and General Workers Union cover many smaller groupings, thus giving greater unity to the labor movement.

Business is badly organized with no all-inclusive powerful organization to represent the interests of the business community as a whole. However, the existence of a number of specialized organizations such as the Federation of Irish Industries and the Federated Union of Employers further indicates that Ireland, unlike many of the nations in the developing areas, today has a system of clearly defined interest organizations. Similarly, agricultural interests are represented by organizations like the important Irish Creamery Milk Suppliers Association and the National Farmers' Association.[38]

Ireland, additionally, has a large number of nationalist organizations. The Sinn Fein Party had since the 1920s become a small, insignificant radical group that sought the reunification of Ireland, the renunciation of economic and political ties with Britain, and, among some members, the socialization of the Irish economy. It also opposed Common Market entry. The illegal Irish Republican Army was prone to sporadic and ineffective campaigns of violence. Of course, the IRA and its political wing, the Sinn Fein Party, have split into official and provisional wings since the recent turbulence in Northern Ireland began. The Provisionals have been of particular significance to the Republic's government because they have used the South as a base of operations for their activities in the North. They oppose the Government of the Republic, and have had an important bearing on relations between the North and South, as well as the United Kingdom. Thus, although there is little active, widespread support for these groups in the Republic, and although the Republic's Government has strong public backing and is in firm control at this point, the Northern issue will, as noted earlier, be discussed later.

A number of organizations exist for the explicit purpose of fostering Gaelic culture. The Gaelic League is the most prominent and important of these organizations and has as its particular purpose, the preservation of the Irish language. It publishes a variety of Irish-language materials, and its program supplements in a very important way the teaching of Irish in the public schools. Recently it has taken a more active political role in such matters as resistance to entry into the Common Market.

Other organizations promote different aspects of Gaelic culture. The Gaelic Athletic Association, for instance, sponsors athletic activities centered around Gaelic games such as hurling and Gaelic football, and plays a prominent role in Irish sports, especially in rural areas. As will be noted in the following chapter, the Gaelic League had a particularly important role in the Independence movement. It is, thus, a significant and continuing organizational component of nationalist sentiment in the Irish political culture.

The Decision-Making Process

Thus far the discussion of Irish politics has centered mainly on political institutions. But this does not in itself provide answers to the really important questions: How are political decisions actually made, and who benefits from the system? It is therefore necessary to examine briefly the processes by which political benefits are allocated in order to assess the democratic quality of politics in Ireland. This chapter will conclude, then, with a brief look at the overall power structure and decision-making process.

One of the major criticisms of Irish government in recent years is that power has become too highly centralized. As we have seen, there is little significant policy making at the local levels, local officials serving mainly as errand runners for their constituents. Deputies and senators perform similar functions, to a very considerable extent, and even the Houses of Oireachtas appear to play a comparatively minor role in the legislative process. Does Ireland, then, possess a Cabinet dictatorship?

To arbitrarily equate centralization with authoritarianism is to foster a misunderstanding of democracy. Current popular and scholarly proposals for decentralization notwithstanding, centralized political leadership does not necessarily mean a lack of democratic control. Especially in a relatively homogeneous society such as the Republic of Ireland, there are a few social diversities based on geographical areas which would justify or, perhaps, compel a need for a more federal distribution of political power.[39] The obverse of the proposition is equally valid: decentralization does not necessarily lead to a greater degree of democracy. It might simply lead to greater domination by local elites. This too can be related to the Irish situation where citizens see councillors as errand runners and where there is little public desire to participate directly in the decision-making process. Of course, regional variations do exist, and administrative decentralization, with some local inputs, can produce greater efficiency. But this does not require local political control. The problem of democratization will be discussed in a later chapter.

Although deputies take little formal role in the policy-making process, the party leaders cannot ignore their wishes; for, given enough provocation, members of the parliamentary party could vote against their leaders. It is therefore clear that the Taoiseach and Cabinet are limited by the anticipated reactions of their supporters.

Perhaps the restraining force of greatest significance, however, is the requirement that public elections be held at least once every five years. Though Irish scholars sometimes criticize the ignorance of the Irish electorate on particular issues, Irish voters are probably at least as knowledgeable as voters in other democratic countries and, perhaps, more so than in most. Irish citizens certainly do not hesitate to make independent judgments. Indeed, Fianna Fáil's efforts to abandon proportional representation, which would probably give the party a greater majority of parliamentary seats, have been rejected by the electorate in constitutional referenda.[40] Because most voters have supported the Fianna Fáil party, their decision to reject the proposed change in the electoral system suggests that Irish citizens do not always follow the wishes of political leaders. The recent defeat of Fianna Fáil in the national elections also suggests a certain voter independence. Further, while the electorate does not have a direct voice in day-to-day decisions, it has an enormous voice from the viewpoint of anticipated reactions. For, clearly, the voters have the power to decide who will form the Government. To be sure, the range of choices open to the electorate may be less than some would prefer, but Irish voters nonetheless have a choice, the fact of which Irish political elites are surely aware.

Yet an increasing number of public-policy decisions are being made by administrative agencies rather than by the Cabinet. The Senate Select

Committee on Statutory Instruments and the Dáil Public Accounts Committee deal with relatively minor matters. Moreover, state-sponsored bodies—while having a major role in Irish society—are subject to fewer limitations than are the government departments. In short, there is a very considerable degree of discretion in the hands of bureaucrats, and thus an inquiry into the character of democracy in Ireland must take into account the extent to which bureaucrats are subject to public control.

A number of constraints do, in fact, exist. First, there is the integrity of Irish administrators, which constitutes a kind of internalized check, for Irish civil servants are honest and have a basically professional outlook. Second, even though the expanding role of government means that many decisions escape the attention of elected politicians, ministers do head government departments and are involved in major policy decisions. Moreover, the laws which provide the legal framework within which administrators can work are passed by democratically elected officials, and these laws greatly limit the possibilities for bureaucratic arbitrariness. Of great significance also, is the ombudsman-like role of the parliamentary deputy, as well as publicity in the mass media. Administrators cannot afford to alienate elected representatives or to arouse consistently the hostility of the public. In short, although Ireland faces the problem common to most Western democratic political systems, namely that of exerting public control over the state's administrative apparatus, a number of significant controls provide a substantial degree of restraint on the bureaucratic system.

Furthermore, interest groups affected by public-policy decisions provide an important check not only on the bureaucracy but also on the elected officials. For example, through advisory bodies, interest groups sometimes play a direct role in the legislative process, particularly in the planning stages of policy making.[41] To be sure, the Government initiates some consultation primarily to gain support, and some major groups, such as the National Farmer's Association, avoid linkages with government agencies in order to have greater freedom of action. But, in the main, group pressures in Ireland constitute an additional control over the public sector.

Groups provide an extra channel of communication between citizen and government, and provide an organized method of voicing complaints if government policy is unfavorable or voicing support if it is favorable. Moreover, not everyone can have an adequate political voice in a system based upon geographic area and majority rule. For instance, an industrial laborer in a rural community or a dentist almost anywhere would be only indirectly represented without group support. Thus, the participation of interest groups in the administrative process increases popular control over Ireland's administrators.[42]

On the other hand, a potential threat to public control in democratic nations is excessive influence by particular groups. Irish writers have often alleged that the Irish Church has had an excessive voice in government affairs. To illustrate, though extensive censorship of political speeches does not exist, censorship of films, plays, and literature is still practiced, not only by bodies employing their own understanding of Catholic morality, but also by the direct intervention of bishops as well. To be sure, the influence of the Church in political affairs is often exaggerated, especially in its clandestine aspects, but the Roman Catholic hierarchy has openly and overtly attempted to influence public-policy decisions by such methods as reading pastoral letters at church services and issuing public statements concerning the Church's position on proposed policies.

The most famous instance in recent years was the Noel Browne affair. As Minister of Health, Browne introduced a proposed mother-and-child scheme whereby the government's role in providing medical care would be extended. Largely because of the open pressure of Irish Catholic bishops against the plan, and partly on the ground that it was an intervention into the family as a social unit, the plan was abandoned and Browne resigned. Of course, the Irish bishops were heavily influenced by pressure from the Irish Medical Association, and Browne himself made some tactical errors in advancing the plan, but the case nevertheless illustrates the point that the Roman Catholic church in Ireland is one of the strongest political forces, outside of government.[43]

Yet several mitigating considerations should be mentioned. First, the small Protestant minority is seldom discriminated against, perhaps because it is relatively wealthy and has considerable resources. Second, the Church has performed an important role through charitable organizations, and has thus relieved the government of a relatively poor country of some of its financial obligations. Also, in a country that is ninety-five percent Catholic, it is fitting that Catholic ethics have an important role in the formation of public policy, as long as the rights of the minority are respected. Finally, attitudes within the Church are becoming more liberal, and the Church has, on the whole, been a constructive as well as a modernizing force in Irish society.[44]

Unlike the military in many transitional societies, the Irish army plays almost no role in the politics of the Irish political system. The military in Ireland is small and receives only a small percentage of the national budget.[45] Its minor role is also indicated by the absence of military officers from government positions of leadership. Even in foreign affairs the policy-making role of the military appears to be negligible.[46]

The central point thus far, then, is that Ireland does in fact have an open and democratic political system. Yet, one final aspect of the system ought to be considered; namely, the matter of who benefits from government decisions. Both major parties have been rather conservative in their orientation toward matters affecting the distribution of economic wealth, and government policy has similarly followed conservative lines. For example, a recent innovation in taxation, the turnover tax, is basically regressive in nature. Also, the distribution of wealth is far from equal, and corporate ownership is concentrated in comparatively few hands.[47]

Furthermore, Irish social services are less extensive than those of most of Western Europe. Although it is steadily expanding the scope of welfare coverage, Ireland does not have a universal or comprehensive scheme of medical care, and only recently instituted financial assistance for the payment of tuition at the secondary school level.[48] A determining factor here is that Ireland does not have a wealthy economic base, and, however desirable progressive taxation may be from a purely social viewpoint, too much of it could hinder efforts directed toward economic development by reducing available investment capital. In fact, tax incentives have been one of the principal means of promoting the growth of the industrial sector. Moreover, the Fianna Fáil party has derived much of its support from small farmers, and, not surprisingly, has promoted a substantial number of programs designed to assist farmers—so much so that one often hears complaints from urban residents about having to pay the bill for these services. Yet, organized labor too is capable of commanding an increasing share of the economic wealth of the country; to the point, indeed, at which inequalities between organized and unorganized labor may become a critical source of injustice in the future.

The present chapter has tried to show that, despite its economic limitations, Ireland possesses a comparatively open, democratic, and effective political system. It will be the task of the next chapter to analyze the processes by which that system was achieved.

3 Irish Political Development: Institutionalization and Social Mobilization

The present chapter will present a historical account of recent Irish political development, using institutionalization and social mobilization as interpretative themes. Institutionalization, it will be recalled, is the process by which government structures and processes acquire value and stability. Therefore, this chapter will be concerned with political culture from the standpoint of the development of public support for the political system. In other words, a study of institutionalization in Ireland necessarily involves a concern with two of the most important dimensions of political culture—the creation of popular feelings of national identity and the development of democratic political values.

Social mobilization is ". . . the process in which major clusters of old social, economic, and psychological commitments are eroded or broken and people become available for new patterns of socialization and behavior."[1] It results from such social forces as urbanization, industrialization, geographic mobility, increased per capita income, and exposure to new ideas through the mass media. Social and economic modernization therefore constitute the principal causes of social mobilization. The significance of social mobilization, for students of political development, is that it places great burdens on governments, especially those governments that have not yet become institutionalized. Social mobilization leads to a higher level of public involvement in politics. It leads to greater demands on government leaders, and creates a need for greatly expanded government services. Increased demands for roads, police, welfare services, and consumer goods illustrate some of these pressures.[2]

Compared with the early stages of modern nations, social mobilization in the Third-World areas of Africa, Asia, and Latin America occurs at a greatly accelerated rate. Because of advanced technology, the process of exposing the citizenry to modern ideas is more rapid and its consequences more telling. Newspapers, movies, radios, and television reach into rural areas. Moreover, unlike the modern nations which had no advanced societies to emulate, the developing countries have modern neighbors as models; this stimulates the desires of public and government alike. Further, not only does social change occur at a more rapid rate in the Third World, but also social and political changes occur simultaneously. Nations like the United States and Britain faced problems such as urbanization, industrialization, and the creation of viable political institutions at different historical periods; they did not have to contend with the existence of electronic media in their earlier stages of development.[3]

The Period Before Independence

Prior to its achievement of independence in 1921, Ireland was for centuries the object of conquest by foreign powers. These attempts at conquest were never quite successful, however, and Ireland has had a history characterized by both violent and peaceful resistance to domination by other nations. About 350 B.C., the island was conquered by the Gaelic Celts. Though the Celts were able to impose their language and much of their culture on the island, their's was not the only influence, for successive invasions by the Scandinavians and Normans also contributed both cultural and racial influences to the later development of Irish society.

Of more immediate importance, because of its impact on Irish political culture, however, was the conquest and domination by the British. Because of its proximity to England, Ireland was not only an attractive target for exploitation, it was also of important strategic consequence for England in its struggle with other European powers. Centuries of conflict between the English and the Irish contributed substantially to the sense of Irish national identity. In spite of the fact that many of the leaders of early nationalist movements were Protestants, there was an important religious dimension in the conflict between the islands. Indeed, repressive policies against Roman Catholics lasted into the nineteenth century. To illustrate, the infamous penal laws provided that Catholics could not maintain public schools, obtain degrees from the University of Dublin, or, for most Catholics, practice law. Moreover, Irish Catholic bishops were expelled in the seventeenth century, and Catholics were prevented from sitting in Irish parliaments or holding government office. The penal laws were not finally repealed until the Catholic emancipation of 1829, and even then some vestiges of discrimination remained.[4]

Agitation for repeal of laws discriminating against Catholics politicized not only mass publics but other sectors of Irish society as well—most obviously the Roman Catholic clergy. Daniel O'Connell and the Catholic Association provided the basis for a mass movement of Catholic Ireland against the British governmental system. Although he sought reform through legal and constitutional means, O'Connell became a hero to Irish Catholics, not only because he advocated their cause, as some liberal Protestants such as Grattan had done, but also because he was himself a Roman Catholic with whom the Catholic public could identify. Even with a highly limited Catholic franchise, Catholics began to win elections to the Westminster Parliament, and O'Connell was himself elected in 1828, although his religion barred him from taking a seat until the passage of the Emancipation Act in 1829. The entrance of Catholics into the British Parliament signaled an important change in the reform movement, for, with 100 Irish parliamentary seats, it became possible for a popularly-based Irish parliamentary party to operate within the legislative system.[5] Parliamentary experience, as well as a gradually expanding electorate, demonstrated to Irish political leaders and to the public that peaceful agitation through parliamentary and legal channels could lead to, at least, some concessions.

But the politicization of the Irish public also became manifest in ways other than formal elections and parliamentary activity. After Catholic emancipation was achieved, the next major political movement led by O'Connell, who was by then known as "the liberator," was for the repeal of the Act of Union with England. The goal of the repeal movement was for Home Rule, by controlling Irish affairs through an Irish parliament, rather than by means of complete separation from England. In any case, in addition to parliamentary activity, O'Connell, through mass rallies called "monster meetings," generated continuing popular support. Thus, further politicization of Irish citizens occurred even though the repeal movement itself failed.[6]

Throughout the nineteenth century political reforms continued to institution-alize democratic political procedures consistent with the British model. In 1840, for example, a municipal reform act made the larger Irish towns more democratic by the abolition of previously corrupt local authorities, and by basing the new councils on elections by property owners. Through acts of Parliament, moreover, Ireland by 1884 achieved a degree of adult suffrage comparable to that of England. The enhancement of democratic processes was particularly assisted by the Local Government (Ireland) Act of 1898, which provided that power formerly in the hands of undemocratic county grand juries now be transferred to county councils, elected on the basis of a broad popular franchise. In sum, by the close of the nineteenth century, the Irish public—like the citizens of England—had achieved significant experience in the electoral process through an expanded franchise and other reforms. Of course, the nineteenth-century reforms also meant that Irish political leaders became accustomed to democratic political procedure, not only in Parliament, but also at the local and administrative levels.[7]

Indeed, one of the most significant developments for Irish political development was the inculcation of professional values in the Irish administrative class. Irish administration, prior to the Act of Union of 1800, was appallingly corrupt. Sinecures, such as the position of "taster of wines" were common, and holders of Irish offices sometimes lived in England. Many officials were paid on the basis of fees rather than salaries, a practice that encouraged many administrative abuses. Yet, the nineteenth century was a period of great reform of the Irish administration. Commissions were appointed to investigate administrative abuses, and many reforms such as the abolition of payment by fees were undertaken. Of particular importance was the appointment of a civil service commission, and, in 1871, the institution of recruitment into the civil service by qualifying examination.[8]

The Irish administration, then, was modernized and changed to a pattern similar to that of Britain but with distinctive features of its own. Although some inefficiencies by the time of independence remained, compared with earlier periods the Irish administration by the 1920s was efficient and was staffed by professionals. Moreover, a large majority of the top administrative positions by 1914 were held by Irishmen. Thus, while Britain was responsible for the establishment of fundamentally rational bureaucratic structures in many of its former colonies, Ireland at independence had the advantage of having a particularly large percentage of high-level positions already filled by Irishmen.[9]

The establishment of democratic political procedures and more rational administrative structures, however, did not make the political system legitimate in the eyes of the Irish. Indeed, even after O'Connell's agitation for Catholic emancipation and for repeal of the Act of Union, political conflict between England and Ireland continued up to the ultimate struggle for independence. Pressure by Irish politicians for home rule was renewed with increased vigor after the advent of Charles Stewart Parnell as leader of the Irish Parliamentary Party. With Gladstone's support there appeared to be a genuine chance of achieving limited home rule through constitutional procedures.

After Parnell's affair with a married woman was exposed, however, he fell from power, largely as the result of denunciation from the Catholic Church. This episode, incidentally, illustrated the continuing importance of the Church in Irish Society. With the fall of Parnell and with the disintegration of the Irish Parliamentary Party, which never again achieved its previous unity and strength, chances for a constitutional settlement dwindled. A number of other political factors were to contribute to the ultimate failure to reach a peaceful solution to the Irish question. The formation of new radical nationalist groups, such as Sinn Féin, with which the more conservative leaders of the Irish party remained unsympathetic, the increasing militancy of the Unionist resistance, and the advent of World War I, all impeded a peaceful settlement.[10]

Controversy in the nineteenth century, however, centered not only on political questions, but also upon profound social issues. Moreover, conflict was not always limited to peaceful constitutional methods; it sometimes surfaced as violent movements against the established order. An abortive nationalist rising in 1798 helped spark the Union of Britain and Ireland, and contributed to an ongoing militantly nationalist spirit that sometimes appeared in unsuccessful rebellions, such as the one of 1803. The problem of the use of land was particularly acute. A system of small tenant holdings without security of tenure, as well as overpopulation, and subsistance or poverty conditions in the towns and rural areas, greatly aggravated the social consequences of the failure of the potato crop—the failure that produced the great famine of 1846 and 1847. Deaths from starvation, resulting from delayed and inadequate assistance from Parliament, were augmented by the spread of diseases such as typhus. The rapid increase in emigration, which was to continue into the twentieth century, was a direct result of the famine. Indeed, a population that stood at over 8,000,000 in 1848 declined by 1911 to 4,390,219, although by then the rate of decline had decreased substantially.[11]

Except for the 1803 and the small, ill-fated rising of the Young Irelanders in 1848, however, nineteenth-century violent confrontations did not appear on a significant scale until the rise of Fenian activity in the 1860s. Like the famine and the resistance of 1848, the Fenian movement resulted in increased national sentiment in Ireland. Three Fenians were executed in 1867 for the death of a British policeman, during a raid on a British jail to release two Fenian leaders, and the "angry feelings in Ireland" which followed led to the holding of processions and mock funerals.[12] The Fenian movement provided impetus toward the disestablishment of the Protestant church in Ireland, and for the first of several land-reform acts which provided for compensation, for improvements, and increased security of tenure. Indeed, with the passage of the Wyndham Act in 1903, the land situation improved— from the condition of poverty-stricken tenancy without significant rights, to a system of private ownership of small farms.[13]

In fact, at the time of independence, despite slow and gradual urbanization, Ireland was still a rural society, most of whose inhabitants had strong roots in their local communities.[14] Thus, pronounced urbanization and geographic mobility, which are often cited as aspects of social mobilization which cause instability, were not to be found in Ireland immediately prior to the final struggle for independence. Emigration also helped reduce potential sources of strain. Nevertheless, individuals remaining in Ireland maintained close ties with relatives in countries such as the United States and Britain. Still, a strong pattern of similarity in social and cultural norms existed between Irish rural and urban residents, thus lessening new urban residents social mobilization.

Despite a traditional pattern of values and a rural society whose inhabitants possessed strong community ties, Ireland was exposed to some modern forms of communication. To be sure, television did not exist at the time of independence, and radio was almost unknown, but the population was remarkably literate and was thus subject to the mobilizing influences of newspapers, pamphlets, and other printed material.

Because of a major program of educational reform begun in the nineteenth century, the Irish system of national elementary schools had nearly eradicated illiteracy by 1910. Even allowing for a degree of error in the census figures of 1911, the point that 3,329,015 of a population of 4,390,219 could read and write indicates a high potential for political communication through printed matter. Indeed, the publications of the Gaelic League played an important part in the final movement for independence.[15]

A significant aspect of Irish educational reform, however, was its apparently deliberate avoidance of things Irish in the national schools. Irish national heroes and Irish culture, including the Irish language, received little attention. Akenson's content analysis of textbook materials of the period indicated not only an avoidance of Irish national issues, but also an attempt to inculcate values of loyalty toward the British political system.[16] Even in the Gaeltaecht areas children were taught to view English as their native language. Nevertheless, the reaction of nationalistic organizations in the early 1900s against the decline of Irish culture was paralleled in some of the national schools, so that by 1910 more elements of Irish culture were included in the school curriculum. The educational system, however, remained fundamentally English, because the British authorities were not willing to alter radically the basic structure of Irish education.[17]

In sum, the nineteenth century and the early part of the twentieth century constituted an age of reform. As the French scholar Paul-DuBois put it, writing prior to the Anglo-Irish War:

The history of Ireland in the nineteenth century is that of a great and slow revolution, at once political and social, by which the English Garrison, the sovereign minority tends to lose its privileges and to return to the ranks, while the majority, the subject people, gradually free themselves and resume their natural rights. The progressive uprising of the Irish people, the simultaneous downfall of the governing classes, is one of the great social facts of contemporary Ireland.[18]

In addition to these major social and political changes that took place under the Union, a number of other more limited social improvements should be noted. Social assistance, most notably old-age pensions and workman's compensation, was instituted under British auspices prior to the 1916 Rising.[19] In fact, Meghen, writing of social programs in County Limerick in the well-known Limerick Survey, maintains that "those years at the beginning of the twentieth century were peaceful ones, during which the gains of the nineteenth century were consolidated."[20] The work of the Rural District Councils resulted, by 1914, in the building of about 4,000 laborers' cottages; also, Council-sponsored road work by direct labor, rather than by contractor, helped ease problems of unemployment.[21] Thus, it seems apparent that a social revolution of major proportions, as well as significant political reforms, occurred prior to the fight for independence.[22]

The Anglo-Irish War

How, then, did an armed fight for independence come about if such significant social and political reforms were being accomplished? Although an extended analysis of the Irish struggle for independence is beyond the scope of the present study, some of the major aspects of that struggle have important implications, not only for Irish political culture, but also for political development under the Free State.

One of the most significant features of the independence movement was the self-conscious attempt to revive Gaelic culture. The Gaelic Revival, led by organizations such as the Gaelic League and the Gaelic Athletic Association, began in the late nineteenth century and reached major proportions by the time of the 1916 Rising. The central theme of the Revival was that Ireland was a distinct cultural nation and that its cultural roots were Gaelic, not English.[23] As a matter of fact, a major impetus to the Gaelic renaissance was the rapid decline of Irish culture during the nineteenth century. The national school system, in particular, was attacked for teaching children to deny their nation.[24] The rapid decline of Irish as the national language during the nineteenth century also was one of the major sources of resentment for leaders such as Douglas Hyde. A literary revival of Gaelic prose and poetry, supplemented by attempts to revive the language, stimulated a renewed interest in the Gaelic tradition. Organizations were formed to encourage the teaching of the Irish language and Irish history in the public schools.[25] Gaelic music festivals were held, and through the Gaelic Athletic Association, Gaelic national pastimes on a massive scale were encouraged, with special emphasis upon Gaelic sports.

An important mystical element, or sense of spiritual link with the Gaelic past, pervaded the Gaelic Revival movement. The revival of the early Irish tale of Cuchulainn, a hero who defended Ireland to the death protecting the "gap of the North" against enemies of his homeland, illustrates the mystical dimension of the effort to revive the ancient Gaelic nation. McCartney is not radically overstating the point when he says that "the image of Cuchulainn strapped to a post and shedding his life's blood in defense of his people, while a torpor hung over their minds, did much to inspire the blood-sacrifice doctrine of the 1916 leaders."[26]

It would, in fact, be difficult to overstate the significance of the Gaelic Revival. Although rooted in centuries of animosity against English rule, the final thrust toward independence, unlike earlier risings, was to a large extent grounded in and motivated by cultural as well as political ideals. The radical Irish political leaders were motivated largely by a strong belief in a distinctly Irish cultural nation. Because of the widespread literacy of the Irish public, it is also possible that the publications of the Gaelic League had some impact on a wider audience than upon the leaders only. Sir Horace Plunkett maintained, in fact, that money to sponsor the programs of the Gaelic League came primarily from the poor, though the precise impact on the mass public cannot be documented.[27] Moreover, while labor movements in other nations in the early twentieth century often had a strong international leaning, the labor movement in Ireland, led by such revolutionary heroes as James Connolly, developed as a strongly nationalistic force against British rule.[28] Furthermore, not only were the leaders of the fight for independence instilled with a strong faith in the cultural identity of the island, but also the sense of national identity was an important component of the political culture of the men who were to become the officials of the future independent state of Ireland, since they were taking part in the independence movement.[29]

Although a detailed discussion of the 1916 Rising and the military conflict prior to independence has no place here, it is worth remarking that at that time many Irish politicians, as well as the majority of Irish citizens, favored nonviolent means of achieving their national goals. The 1916 Rising involved a force of only about 2,000 men. Only the Dublin General Post Office and other key areas were seized. The Rising was limited to a relatively small segment of the radical nationalist leaders, and the declining Nationalist parliamentary party was not involved in the incident. The insurrection itself was defeated by British forces after six days of fighting, and the principal leaders of the Rising, including Patrick Pearse and James Connolly, were executed.

Public sentiment at first was against the Rising, but the execution of the leaders and the mass imprisonments produced an enormous change in public opinion, especially when considered in light of later attempts at conscription. Indeed, the leaders of the insurrection became national heroes, and in Ussher's slight overstatement, ". . . their photographs, on a popular series of postcards, adorned every mantlepiece in the country."[30] General Maxwell, who was commander of the British forces during this period, maintained that:

. . . from one cause or another a revulsion of feeling set in—one of sympathy for the rebels. Irish M.P.'s, the press, priests, and public bodies have, by their actions, increased this feeling, with the result that the executed leaders have become martyrs, and the rank and file "patriots."[31]

The principal Irish advocates of peaceful change, the members of the Nationalist party, had by this time become unpopular with the public, as well as with the members of the radical nationalist organizations.[32] There seemed to be little hope of a peaceful solution, especially in view of the intransigence of the Unionists, the continuing delay in the implementation of the Home Rule Bill, and the increasing feelings of distrust and hostility of the Irish public toward British policies in Ireland. For British policies contributed to the alienation of the Irish public after the Rising. Attempts to conscript Irish troops were particularly ill-advised. The Irish clergy openly opposed the measure, and the number of volunteers for the Irish Republican Army increased. Even the usually more conservative Church hierarchy denounced the conscription measures of 1918 as unlawful.[33] Although the British abandoned their attempts to implement conscription, the damage was done.

At the parliamentary elections of December, 1918, the Sinn Féin party, of the republican forces, won 73 of the Irish seats. Those members of Sinn Féin who were elected, and were not in jail, refused to take their seats in London. Instead, they formed a parliament of their own, the Dáil Eireann, and met in Dublin in January, 1919, to form a new Irish government. Gradually, the authority of the anti-British government spread throughout the country, with the result that after 1918 there existed two competing governments in Ireland.[34]

To sum up, increased fighting after 1918 led to a full-fledged guerrilla war against the British, in which public support further solidified behind the republican forces as a result of British repression. After the Home Rule Act was passed in 1920, dividing the island into two political units, the republican and British leaders finally reached an agreement in London in December 1921 which provided for an Irish Free State with Dominion status. Six northern counties in Ulster, representing the heavily Protestant and Unionist section of the island, retained their ties with Britain with the result that a central feature of the treaty was the temporary, at least, acceptance of partition.[35]

The struggle for independence was primarily a political rather than social movement. It was noted earlier that a major program of land reform took place prior to the 1916 Rising, and that the preceding century had witnessed a variety of political and administrative reforms. Many of these reforms served to politicize the Irish public and thus increase the sources of support available to Irish political leaders. The efforts to mobilize support in the struggle for ownership of the land, for example, resulted not only in land reform, but also left a better-organized rural citizenry, freer to concentrate on nationalistic concerns, once land reform was achieved.[36] Thus, the British policy of "killing Home Rule by kindness" increased the ability of Irish revolutionary elites to mobilize popular support against British rule. The principal factors leading up to an armed struggle, then, were mainly nationalistic, cultural, and political rather than social—although many of the roots of that struggle undoubtedly lay in some of the earlier social injustices.[37]

Political Development After Independence

With the partitioning of Ireland, the new Free State Government was deprived of the city of Belfast and some of the most economically advanced sections of the island, and faced the tasks of economic development and reconstruction after the war against the British without those resources. On the other hand, the loss of the six counties of Northern Ireland relieved the new Government of having to deal with those inhabitants who were most opposed to the idea of an independent Irish nation. Furthermore, according to the 1926 census, the new Irish state had a population composed of 92.6 percent Roman Catholics, which meant that the religious environment of the political system was homogeneous.[38] Moreover, because religious minorities were guaranteed freedom of religion by the new constitution, and, because Protestants were a relatively privileged sector of Irish society, the religious problem posed little threat to the new political system. Additionally, aside from negative sentiments toward the former members of the political establishment, there was little class conflict in Irish society. As noted above, for example, there was little class content in the fight for independence, for even though the republican forces obtained less support from wealthy farmers, businessmen, and other more privileged sectors of Irish society, the nationalist forces drew support from most groups and classes, and that support increased in all quarters as the rebellion against British rule continued. Thus, despite particularly strong support from the poorer parts of rural Ireland, the insurrection soon acquired a broad-based following.

Nevertheless, the new Free State Government faced formidable problems. The dispute with Northern Ireland over the boundary between the partitioned sectors continued until the issue was resolved in 1925, with an agreement on the original boundary delineating the six counties in the North. Moreover, between 1911 and 1926 the population continued to decline, with some of the most highly-trained people leaving the nation.[39] Yet the emigration of more highly-trained persons from Ireland drained off important potential sources of discontent. In other words, many of the people who left at independence were unsympathetic with the new government. Moreover, many of those who left could not have found suitable employment in Ireland. To the extent that they would have been hostile to the Irish government, emigration reduced the strain on the political system. Nonetheless, the loss of skilled personnel in the newly-emergent poor nation must be viewed as an economic and social liability.

The Government of this heavily agricultural new nation had to contend with a series of bad harvests, a problem that was compounded—because of the conclusion of World War I and the loss of wartime markets—by declining prices for agricultural produce. The fishing industry, also affected by the decline of war-level prices, suffered a similar setback. A particularly acute problem was rising unemployment:

None of the many difficulties that contributed to the chaos in which the Free State was born, has caused more anxiety to the Government or done so much to provide common ground for those who were discontented, as the heavy burden of unemployment.[40]

A number of forces contributed to the problems of rising unemployment, including the return of Irish soldiers who served under the British during the war, and the reduction in the size of the Irish army after domestic hostilities concluded.

If social problems were serious, political issues were monumental. With the formation of the Free State the country was plunged into civil war. The principal immediate cause was the refusal of some of the leaders, most notably Eamon de Valera and part of the Irish armed forces, to accept the provisions of the Treaty. Particularly odious to the anti-Treaty leaders was the required oath of "faithfulness" to the British king, and, less significantly, the retention of British naval bases on Irish soil. To some, the partitioning of the island was also crucial. But the Treaty had been negotiated by representatives of the Irish; it had been approved by the Dáil; and, in popular elections held after the Dáil approval of the Treaty, the pro-Treaty forces defeated the republicans and won a substantial majority of the seats. The results at the June elections, however, were not accepted by the republicans as legitimate or binding, and fighting broke out between the Government and the republicans.[41]

While the scope of the fighting was limited, the events of the Civil War still affect contemporary Irish politics. The fighting itself was brief; the heaviest conflicts were over by the end of the year. Yet the bitterness generated by the Civil War placed a great strain on the early years of parliamentary democracy and helped shape politics in Ireland for decades to come. On the government side, Michael Collins, head of the army, was killed in an ambush by republican forces. Republican prisoners, on the other hand, were sometimes executed after trial by court martial and, in at least one instance, without trial. By June, 1923, the Minister for Home Affairs claimed that twelve thousand or more republican prisoners were under military detention.[42]

For a number of reasons, including weariness from fighting and the legitimacy accorded to the Government by the Dáil votes and by popular elections, public sympathies were generally not on the side of the republicans, especially after the Government proved itself capable of governing. This is not to say that the Free State Government was immediately popular or was viewed with affection by Irish citizens; it was, after all, partially the product of British policy. One may suggest, however, that the republican failure to defeat the Government through guerrilla military operations was, at least in part, due to public sentiment. Moreover, the hierarchy of the Roman Catholic church supported the Government, as it had for the most part under the British, and urged citizens to obey the civil authorities.[43]

Hence, unlike many emergent nations, Ireland faced an attempt by dissatisfied elements to overthrow the newly independent government. In Ireland, however, the attempt failed, and by the end of the summer of 1923 the insurrection gradually ended. To be sure, an abortive military coup by some of the officers of the Irish Army in 1924 could have created a dangerous precedent, but with the retirement or dismissal of some of the disaffected elements, and with the reduction in size of the military after the Civil War, the military by the 1930s had become a small and, largely, depoliticized force in Irish society.[44]

After hostilities ceased de Valera and the republicans challenged the Government party, Cumann na nGaedheal (later to become Fine Gael), at Dáil elections. But the republicans (later to become the Fianna Fáil party), won only a minority of seats in the Dáil, and refused to take the oath of allegiance to the British king. In 1927 Cosgrave's Government introduced a bill barring candidates from running for seats in the Dáil, unless they took an oath promising to assume their places in the Dáil if elected. De Valera and Fianna Fáil then agreed to take the oath, calling it an empty formula and promising to abolish it when they came to power, a promise which they eventually fulfilled. It was not until the 1932 elections, however, that Fianna Fáil, with the support of the Labour party, finally assumed power.

As Frank Munger's analysis of the 1932 elections has demonstrated, the change of Government was a major landmark in the political development of the independent, democratic Irish state. Although the army was small, it still had power sufficient to prevent the accession of de Valera and his supporters, whom it had fought in the Civil War. Munger notes, however, that in addition to the reduced strength of the army, and its gradual professionalization after the retirement of some of its more politically-oriented members, there also existed a strong democratic basis in recruitment policies. Thus, "because the army was a cross section of the general public, it shared the same political culture as the general public. That culture assumed the subordination of the military to the political."[45]

Munger's analysis also suggests that Cosgrave and his Government did not plan the use of force to prevent de Valera's taking office—this despite the bitter animosities that still existed between the two parties. It is significant that de Valera did not plan any revolutionary alterations. However, there were radical overtones to his program, including the division of large farms, greater separation from Britain (e.g., abolishing the oath of allegiance), and the release of political prisoners. Nevertheless, there was no threat of a total overthrow of social institutions, and the major changes were political, not social.

The 1930s was a period of stress. Nonetheless, the overall impact of the period contributed to the institutionalization of democratic structures and processes; that is, by weathering the stresses of the period democratic institutions increased their resilience, adaptability, and indicated their deep penetration of the Irish political culture. For example, the rise of the semi-fascist Blueshirts as a mass movement in the 1930s and the continued violence perpetrated by the illegal Irish Republican Army were quite significant. Nevertheless, the IRA was firmly and effectively limited by the Government. Similarly, the Blueshirts did not quite develop sufficient public support to become a serious threat to existing democratic institutions, and, as Maurice Manning shows, were not so extremist as their Continental counterparts. Indeed, their moderation compared with, say, the Nazis, was in no small measure due to their alliance with two constitutional parties, Cummann na nGaedheal and The Centre Party.[46] In short, the majority of Irishmen continued to abide by democratic procedures and to support elected officials.

Irish politicians had to deal with some conflicts in international politics, especially with Great Britain. But the conflict between Ireland and Britain strengthened Irish national sentiment and resulted in additional support for the support for the political leaders, in spite of British reprisals. To illustrate, in 1932 de Valera's policies of further breaking ties with Britain led to economic reprisals. When de Valera refused to allow further payments to Britain of land-purchase annuities, the British retaliated with tariffs on Irish agricultural products. Although economic conditions worsened, the Fianna Fáil party continued to win the support of the Irish public at elections, and de Valera continued his policy of breaking the remaining ties with Britain. The culmination of this policy was the adoption of a new constitution in 1937, the one still in force today. Among other things, that constitution changed the name of the nation from the Irish Free State to Eire or Ireland. Ironically, it was a coalition Government, headed by John Costello and the Fine Gael party, that formally adopted by statute in 1949 the new title "Republic of Ireland."

The Constitution of 1937 made several key structural changes in the Irish government. It is, therefore, of interest to describe some of the major features of the original constitution and to indicate briefly their significance. Under the conditions of the Treaty, which of course partly determined the content of the Free State Constitution, the new Free State was to have Dominion status. Thus, instead of a president there was a governor-general representing the British monarch and, at least technically, appointed by him. In accordance with Commonwealth practice, however, the choices of the governor-general from the first days of the Free State were made by the Irish Government, and they were Irishmen. Furthermore, the holder of the office of governor-general of the Irish Free State naturally had substantially less power than that of the president after 1937. Additionally, with respect to legislative powers, and external powers in dealing with members of the Commonwealth, the role of the governor-general was, of course, almost entirely formal.

More interesting was the experiment with what were called the "extern" ministers. In an attempt to avoid some of the features of the British system, especially the centralized power of the Cabinet and central role of parties, the framers of the constitution provided for "extern" ministers who were to be appointed individually by the Dáil, and were to be individually responsible to it rather than to the executive. Yet the original proposals were not adopted, and the final version of the constitution gave the extern ministers more limited powers. The Executive Council dominated Dáil politics from the beginning: for, in practice, political realities created a need for strong government in the first stages of the Free State's existence; and later realities, namely the existence of strongly opposed groups within the Dáil, led to a system of strong party government. Thus, from the start, Ireland possessed an executive council similar in operation to the British Cabinet, and the extern ministers, who were supposed to be individually responsible to the Dáil, never achieved an important role in Irish politics.[47]

A final, interesting experiment of the new Free State Constitution was the effort to facilitate direct legislation through initiative and referendum. By a request of either two-fifths of the Dáil or a majority of the Senate, a bill passed by the Oireachtas (other than a money or an emergency bill), was suspended for ninety days. During this period, a referendum could then be demanded either by three-fifths of the Senate or by a petition signed by at least one-twentieth of the registered voters. The referendum itself required only a majority of those voting to determine the bill's passage or rejection. The significance of these procedures is that referenda could be demanded with comparative ease, and that merely a majority of those voting could decide the issue. Thus, at least in theory, direct popular control was greatly facilitated.

However, the initiative and referendum procedures were never employed in practice, because of the realities of party politics and the emergency conditions facing the new Government. In any case, initiative and referenda are incompatible with the principles of responsible parliamentary (party) government. The procedures were dropped in 1928 by Government legislation when the minority Fianna Fáil party appealed to the public to override the Government position on the oath of allegiance.[48] In summation, then, although the Free State possessed constitutionally-defined procedures and structures which could have provided it with political institutions differing substantially from the British model, in practice the similarities of the two systems were great. And these similarities were retained in the 1937 Constitution and have continued to the present, as indicated in the preceding chapter.

The Civil Service

A major reason for the failure of many new nations to develop politically is the lack of honest and efficient civil servants. The new Free State Government, however, did not have this problem. The reform of the Irish administration during the Union with the British led to a professional administrative system, staffed even at the highest levels by Irishmen. But these administrators were employees of the British and, thus, might have been viewed by the new Free State Government and by the public as remnants of a hated foreign regime. In that case, cooperation between bureaucrats and elected officials would have been impeded. In fact, the new regime might have had to attempt the complex task of rebuilding the administrative system.

Few changes were made, however, in the crucial matter of administrative personnel. This can be attributed partly to the political settlement between

Britain and the Irish forces, for the

. . . transferred officers carried with them into their new sphere of activity certain rights expressly conferred on them under the Treaty of the 6th of December, 1921, whereby their future tenure and conditions of employment were protected in certain respects and provision was made for compensation in the event of retirement.[49]

Yet, despite the option of retirement afforded by Article 10 of the Treaty, of 21,000 employees transferred to the control of the Irish Free State Government only 1,405 retired between 1922 and 1934.[50]

Of course, some changes were necessary because several of the departments under the Union maintained their central offices in London rather than in Dublin. New head offices had to be established in Dublin for the Department of Finance and for the Post Office. Furthermore, some totally new administrative departments had to be created. The Free State Government formed entirely new organizations for handling defence and external affairs. Yet because of the highly developed administrative apparatus inherited by the Government of the newly independent state, the immediate expansion of the civil-service staffs added only about 1,000 persons by October, 1923. In short, because of the existence of a modern administrative system, and particularly because of the successful transfer of a professional civil service, especially at the higher ranks, the institutionalization of the public bureaucracy was a relatively simple matter for the Irish Free State.[51] In this respect Ireland had a distinct advantage over many of the nations that gained independence in the twentieth century, even those that were under British rule. For in many such countries, top-level positions were filled by English administrators.

The Development of a Democratic Political Culture

As Brian Farrell has pointed out, a crucial and interesting feature of the Irish agitation against British domination was its legal and constitutional character.[52] Grattan's efforts in the Irish Parliament, prior to the Union, O'Connell's struggles for Catholic representation in the British Parliament after the Union, Parnell and the Nationalist party's efforts to achieve home rule by means of parliamentary agitation—these and other constitutional activities created in Irish political leaders a strong preference for democratic government. Indeed, many of the Free State leaders experienced democratic politics directly. Although relatively few of them were members of the British Parliament in London, many of the nationalist leaders had had experience in democratic procedures at the local levels.[53]

One of the clearest indications of the values of Irish leaders is the Constitution of the Irish Free State. It clearly shows a strong preference for democratic procedures. Indeed, in the words of Leo Kohn, "an intense democratic radicalism permeates the framework of the Irish Constitution."[54] That democratic commitment can be seen in many ways. A system of extern ministers was provided to circumvent the concentration of power in the hands of a cabinet. The usual guarantees of civil liberties and rights were provided for, although sometimes with escape clauses. Thus, "the dwelling of each citizen is inviolable and shall not be forcibly entered except in accordance with law."[55] Similarly, the Constitution provided for freedom of expression and freedom of assembly; no title of honor could be conferred, and universal suffrage was assured.[56] In short, except for some of the unique features noted earlier, the Constitution of the Irish Free State was a typically democratic constitutional document, and this democratic spirit was of course carried over into the Constitution of 1937.

Yet not all of the evidence indicates a clear adherence to democratic values. We have already alluded to the Civil War and the abortive military coup of 1924. The statements of de Valera preceding the Civil War also reflect a quite imperfect commitment to constitutional democracy among the anti-Treaty leaders. For example, de Valera said that "Republicans maintain. . . that there are rights which a minority may justly uphold, even by arms, against a majority."[57]

After the Fianna Fáil party entered the Dáil, a number of statements by party leaders also appeared at first glance to augur poorly for the future development of a democratic political system. Thus, the future Taoiseach, Sean Lemass, stated:

I think it would be right to inform Deputy Davin that Fianna Fáil is a slightly constitutional party. We are perhaps open to the definition of a constitutional party, but before anything we are a Republican party. We have adopted the method of political agitation to achieve our end, because we believe, in the present circumstances, that method is best in the interests of the nation and of the Republican movement, and for no other reason.[58]

Later in the debate over the release of Civil War prisoners, Lemass maintained that "our object is to establish a Republican Government in Ireland. If that can be done by the present methods we have we will be very pleased, but if not we would not confine ourselves to them."[59] Yet, de Valera was perhaps a bit more moderate in his statement:

As far as I am concerned, the only Constitution I give "that" for, the only thing I think I am morally bound to obey in this House, is a majority vote, because you are all elected by the Irish people. As a practical rule, and not because there is anything sacred in it, I am prepared to accept majority rule as settling matters of national policy, and therefore as deciding who it is that shall be in charge of order.[60]

It must be remembered, however, that feelings were unusually bitter after the Civil War, and that, from the point of view of Fianna Fáil, the Government obtained its potision illegally and, thus, constituted an illegitimate majority in the Dáil. Hostilities gradually declined, however, and the number of radical statements gradually subsided.[61] Not only did the Cosgrave Government allow a peaceful transition of power in 1932, but also de Valera and the Fianna Fáil party permitted the formation of a coalition Government in 1948. In fact, from its first days in office, Fianna Fáil tended to respect the political freedoms of its parliamentary opponents. To be sure, through military tribunals and other means, party members cracked down hard on radical organizations like the Blueshirts and the Irish Republican Army, sometimes ignoring usual constitutional procedures. But, given the bitterness and fervent attitudes generated by the Anglo-Irish and Civil Wars, as well as the policies of these radical groups, their actions were understandable if not always justifiable. Moreover, the overall impact of their policies by 1937 (and especially by World War II, with its unifying consequences). was to contribute further to democratic institutionalization.

Social and Economic Values

Since the 1920s, both major parties, and to a degree the Labour party, have been rather conservative. The Labour party, of course, favored policies that would strengthen the Labour movement, but it was not radically socialistic, and the Fianna Fáil party favored smaller farmers more than did Cosgrave's party. Nevertheless, none of the three major parties favored radical social changes in Irish society. It should be noted, however, that the socialist element in Labour's thought and politics became increasingly significant in the 1960s.

On the other hand, both major parties supported limited state-intervention in the economy for purposes of industrial growth and public welfare. The first Free State Government assumed responsibility for the economic well-being of the society, and viewed economic regulation as a legitimate end of government.[62] But the Government also took a more positive approach to the promotion of economic welfare by actively sponsoring developmental programs such as the Shannon River electrification project and the building of major public works. The Cosgrave Government and the de Valera Government, as well, used regulatory protective tariffs for the purpose of assisting the establishment of native industries. In the case of Fianna Fáil, however, the tariffs were a response to the actions of the British government.[63] In sum, though preferring a capitalist economic system, early Irish governments never felt bound to entirely laissez faire economic policy. They were not, however, radically democratic in their social policies, and did not seek to alter fundamentally the distribution of economic wealth.

Popular Attitudes and Values

Attention has centered thus far on the beliefs and values of political leaders. It is also important, however, to discuss the development of democratic values among the public. Beginning in the nineteenth century, the Irish public participated in various ways in democratic political processes. Electoral reform, and especially reform of local government, gave democratic political experience to the citizenry. The mass movements of the nineteenth century aimed for the most part at achieving such reforms as the removal of discrimination against Catholics in politics. "In the consciousness of the people the anti-democratic had ever been identical with the anti-national, however little indeed such identification might frequently have corresponded to actual facts."[64]

Even more significant was the popular acceptance of the Free State Government during and after the Civil War. Had the great majority of the public strongly supported de Valera and the republicans, it is unlikely that the new Government could have survived. Of great importance is the fact that much of the Government's legitimacy resulted from its victory in democratic elections and its majority support in the Dáil. In short, the Irish public valued democratic processes, or at least supported parties that espoused democratic values.

This support of democratic political procedures has continued up to the present. According to the government-sponsored 1967 *Report of the Committee on the Constitution:*

. . . the republican status of the State, national sovereignty, the supremacy of the people, universal franchise, fundamental rights such as freedom of speech, association, and religion, the rule of law and equality before the law, were all part and parcel of this nation's struggle for independence and it is not surprising, prehaps, that, in the minds of the people, they are now to be regarded as virtually unalterable.[65]

In sum, institutionalization, that is the processes by which political structures and procedures acquire value and stability, was substantially completed prior to the establishment of the Irish Free State. Naturally, a fundamental institutional change was involved in the shift of authority from London to Dublin. But basic political procedures such as universal franchise, freedom of speech, and other civil rights and liberties, were already valued by most of the political leaders and the public. Moreover, Irish Free State institutions closely followed the model of the British parliamentary system, and the bureaucracy and civil service, including top-level native administrators, were transferred almost completely intact to the new Irish Government. Thus, the often critical problem in new nations of establishing and maintaining viable political institutions was for Ireland a manageable task. The Civil War, of course, constituted a critical challenge to the institutional structures and procedures of the new political system, but the Government successfully weathered this stormy, but largely ineffectual, protest to its legitimacy.

Social Mobilization

Irish governments have had comparatively few problems compared with those of the recently established nations. Indeed, the period of greatest social change occurred after World War II. Extensive exposure to modern values, the introduction of television, rapid economic development, and other major social changes are a recent phenomenon.

The most crucial feature of social change in Ireland, with respect to possible strains on the political system, has been its sequential and extended character. As indicated earlier, the system of public schools produced a literate public well before the 1916 Easter Rising. Moreover, participation in mass political movements and experience in democratic political procedures were not new to the citizens of the Irish Free State. Exposure to "modernity" was obviously not as sudden for the Irish citizens as it was for the nations that have gained independence in recent years. Modern means of communications developed gradually, and television did not even exist during the initial years of independence. Thus, some types of social change occurred well before independence, while other changes occurred at a gradual rate.

In addition, since the 1850s Ireland has not faced the problem of a rapidly growing population, and until quite recently it remained a provincial and essentially rural society with moderate internal geographic mobility.[66] Even today rural inhabitants account for nearly half of the population. Also, as noted in the last chapter, the bulk of Irish exports consist of agricultural products.

Furthermore, much of the geographic mobility that evolved took the form of emigration to foreign nations. Because few well-paying jobs existed, emigration drained off potential sources of discontent even though some needed professionals were also lost. Moreover, economic and political difficulties during and after the Civil War, and through the depression years, produced a rate of economic growth so slow that few of the strains of a rapidly expanding economy developed. Finally, urbanization proceeded at a much slower pace than in many new nations.[67]

Conclusion

Social mobilization was a continuing, though not simultaneous, process which, in its important aspects, began early in the nineteenth century. Thus, social stresses confronting the new Irish governments were manageable when compared with the devastating rapidity of simultaneous social changes confronting the newly emergent nations.

With respect to the relations between political culture and political development, a matter that is of treat concern in the present study, only two dimensions have been dealt with in the present chapter—namely, the dimensions of national identity, and of democratic political values. It has been noted that experience in democratic procedures during the nineteenth and early twentieth centuries constituted a source of legitimacy for the new Free State Government. This early experience, of course, also facilitated the task of developing peaceful and effective public participation.

Yet, national identity needs some further elaboration, for it is this aspect of political culture that is basic to any kind of political development, whether democratic or authoritarian. A theme of the present chapter has been, indeed, the point that through the repeated struggles against British domination of the island, a strong sense of national identity developed. When it is recalled that hostility toward foreign rule was supplemented by a strong cultural emphasis on Irish nationalism in the independence movement, it is clear that a strong sense of national identity gave an important reserve of popular support for the new state. Thus, from the standpoint of both democratic and nationalist sentiments, the Irish political culture facilitated the institutionalization processes in the founding of the Irish nation.

Yet Lucian Pye is correct in maintaining that the style of interaction among persons is of major importance in considering the prospects for political development in new nations.[68] Therefore, a crucial dimension in the study of political culture and political development is the determination whether or not citizens trust one another and can enter into relations which facilitate the development of organizations. Implicit in the preceding two chapters is the observation that, at least within the formal electoral and parliamentary processes, interpersonal relations did not cause a breakdown in the operation of the democratic polity. And that raises something of a problem, for it is quite clear (as will be demonstrated in the following chapters) that Irish social institutions and political activities are often authoritarian and highly personalistic.

A major assumption in much of the political-science literature has been that authoritarian and personalistic social and political values are harmful for democratic political development, and are more typical of dictatorial, corrupt, or inefficient political systems. It remains, then, to analyze in more detail the dimensions of personalism and authoritarianism in the Irish political culture, and to inquire how they can be reconciled with the evident commitment to democratic structures and values.

4 Irish Authoritarianism

Human relations are frequently a serious impediment to political development. Even where no cultural divisions fragment a nation, the inability of people to get along prevents the development of flexible and effective organizations. It also impedes democratic development because people do not trust one another. Nor is this problem limited exclusively to Third-World areas.

In his study of a community in Southern Italy, Edward Banfield described an extremely hostile social environment. Practically no extended family-system existed, and people outside of the nuclear family were viewed with great distrust. In fact, citizens accepted cheating and, even, stealing if it helped one's immediate family. Banfield called this "amoral familism." It is hardly surprising that, in this setting, it was almost impossible to create and maintain effective organizations. Because people did not trust the motives and actions of others, they believed that anyone engaged in politics was interested solely in enriching himself. Effective development of a democratic system of politics was therefore impossible.[1]

Ireland, however, was blessed by a far more cohesive system of human relations; one, indeed, which provides the major social foundation for its successful democratic political development. Two of the most pronounced features of Irish culture will provide the framework for this discussion; namely, authoritarianism, and, as discussed in the following chapter, personalism.

One of the implications of the traditional literature in political science is that authoritarian social values endanger democratic institutions and procedures. Deference and obedience toward the head of the family, for example, have been said to encourage deference and obedience toward political leaders and, hence, to increase the potential for dictatorship. Authoritarian social values in Germany, for instance, were sometimes used as the basis for a plausible, though not necessarily correct, explanation of the rise of Nazism.

On the other hand, one of the principal themes in the more recent literature is the possible utility of traditional values, even those of an authoritarian nature.[2] More specifically, in the long run even the development of democratic structures and processes can be aided by social behavior that is authoritarian. Obedience and deference can help maintain political stability during the initial phases of nation building, because people will be more willing to accept the government's actions as legitimate. Of course, political stability facilitates the institutionalization of parties, interest groups, and the government itself.

Most attention has been placed on the consequences for political systems, rather than on the implications for organizations. Yet, the capacity of nations to create efficient organizations is crucial in determining a nation's chances for successful political development.[3] Bureaucracies in the developing nations are typically overstaffed and corrupt. Furthermore, political leaders often lose control of unwieldy agencies, whose members are more committed to enriching themselves and their friends than to obeying political leaders who seek reform.[4]

This chapter will survey the authority patterns of the major social systems of Irish society, and analyze their significance to the political development of Ireland. The analysis will emphasize the implications of these patterns for the development of effective organizations, as well as political institutions. The term "authority" refers to the ability of persons to make binding decisions affecting others, and to the beliefs and values that support the particular decision-making pattern. The term "authoritarian" refers to a particular class of authority relations in which the decision-making roles of persons are structured in a significantly hierarchical manner. Therefore, in an authoritarian system one or more persons make decisions that normally are not subject to the veto of others. The term "authoritarian" will also refer to the values supporting this type of system.

Of course, authority is seldom unlimited because people in subordinate positions must be willing to obey. Power relations are therefore reciprocal, even in authoritarian systems. Therefore, the terms "authoritarian" and "non-authoritarian" (or democratic) do not refer to polar terms; instead, they are descriptive terms denoting predominant tendencies within particular social systems. Moreover, there are a number of components and possible dimensions of authoritarianism, including respect for authority, obedience, male-female relations, and religious values.

Authority in Irish Society

Throughout Irish history, social institutions have been highly authoritarian, and most remain substantially so today despite the successful development of a democratic political system. Even in the early Celtic social systems, authority was essentially hierarchical although limited elections sometimes took place.[5] Social and political life in more recent times was also authoritarian. As was suggested in an earlier chapter, feelings toward political leaders like Daniel O'Connell, who were themselves in the vanguard of the struggle for political democracy, were strongly emotional and authoritarian. Indeed, Horace Plunkett, in the early part of this century, wrote that

. . . the political leaders are seen to enjoy an influence over the great majority of the people which is probably as powerful as that of any political leaders in ancient or modern times. . . .[6]

Plunkett's point, if somewhat overstated, nevertheless illustrates public attitudes that might easily have been exploited by politicians not committed to a democratic system of politics.

Still, partly as a result of hostility to British officials, a kind of perverse popular ambivalence toward authority developed in Ireland, at least with respect to the government. Public officials, as well as citizens, willingly ignored laws and regulations that seemed to serve no immediate purpose. The police have been, perhaps, more flexible and humane than other public employees in their treatment of people. Interestingly, Irish-American police tend to be more personalistic in their approach than are other American police.[7] Most Dubliners, moreover, expect fair treatment from police officials.[8]

Yet public ambivalence toward law reflects not so much an unwillingness to accept authority as an unwillingness to accept regimentation. For, if such a thing as an Irish "character" exists, it manifests itself by an unwillingness to tolerate rigorous discipline—a trait that is difficult to measure, but nevertheless quite real. The political significance of this point is that resistance to regimentation would not preclude the development of an authoritarian dictatorship, although it would impede the development of a highly regimented system, like that of Nazi Germany. But the significance of this resistance should not be carried too far. In dealing with the issue of whether or not the Irishman is an extreme individualist, Connery noted that, despite a certain bent in this direction, "It seems to me just as true to say that he is a great conformist who is only too ready to accept authority and deride those who break with convention. Perhaps the balance is that within a rigid framework of conformity (for he is one of the most conservative of beings), the Irishman revels in his obstinacy."[9]

The Irish Family

The most fundamental and significant social system for the study of Irish political beliefs and values is the family. Studies concerned with socialization demonstrate that major political beliefs come from the family setting, and that basic values such as feelings toward political leaders are formed by early adolescence.[10] The importance of the Irish family is unusually great. Arensberg and Kimball showed the family to be the most significant social unit in the area of rural Ireland they studied.[11] Of course, Hannan has since demonstrated the existence of other important social networks, and Arensberg and Kimball may have overstated the positive dimensions of social life.[12] But there is no question that rural family ties were extremely pronounced and generally cohesive. Humphreys has pointed out, moreover, that kinship patterns in Dublin are as strong as in any urban setting in the Western world.[13]

What particular authority patterns characterize this social system so central to Irish society? One of the most significant characteristics is male dominance. Within the home the major decisions are traditionally made by the male head-of-family, whose word—especially in economic matters—is absolute. "Although the father does not take a very active part in family life, he is, nevertheless, an autocrat, and his word, when he chooses, is law."[14]

To be sure, since independence the dominant role of fathers has been growing less authoritarian, especially in urban areas, although, compared with many democratic nations, parents retain a strong voice in the lives of their children.[15] Especially today, Irish fathers leave important decisions to their wives. Matters of education and marriage, in particular, are settled by the Irish wife and mother.[16] Yet fathers still command substantial respect.

Male predominance goes even further. Sons also command deference from the females in the family. Even mothers display deference toward their sons and require, also, that their daughters "slave" for their brothers.[17] Indeed, according to McNabb, there remains even today an "Oriental" attitude toward girls in the family, which is to say that while female children are loved they are placed, nevertheless, in a secondary and less favored position within the Irish family.[18]

Another feature of Irish family life that is important in discussing family authority patterns is the practice of matchmaking. Choosing marriage partners for sons and daughters, usually based on such criteria as wealth, land, and social status, has long been an important feature of Irish society. Though the practice is virtually dead today, it characterized Irish society during the early part of the century and during the crucial early stages of nation building. Indeed, as Robert Lynd pointed out in 1909, daughters' marriages were frequently arranged without reference to their wishes. But the point should not be carried too far, for, even if girls did not choose husbands, they often could veto men they did not wish to accept as husbands.[19] In sum, then, particularly during the first half of the century, authority relations in Irish families displayed a substantial degree of male dominance. Even today, "the mature, adult woman has a specific place in the community and she knows it and keeps is. This is, briefly, at home looking after her husband, house and family."[20]

A related feature of authority in Irish families, and indeed, the community at large, is great respect for the aged. The status accorded to the aged has been more than honorific, for the elder members of the communities, particularly in small-town and rural settings, were sometimes the most important community decision-makers. To illustrate, the old men of the community often determined local public opinion through gossip in informal groups. Thus, in spite of the fact that local elections have been held since the last century, community life nonetheless was frequently authoritarian until quite recently, in part due to the prominent role of older men.[21]

Age is similarly venerated within the nuclear family. Irish children treat their parents with great respect, and, as O'Danachair points out, this respect continues long after children become adults.[22] This deference to age, moreover, is matched by the remarkably slow process by which Irish children mature. In part because of their sheltered lives, and in part because they make few important decisions in life until a relatively late age, Irish men and women in their late teens and early twenties, especially Irish women, often seem immature and lacking in self-sufficiency. Indeed, in rural areas men and women in their thirties and forties are sometimes still referred to as "boys" or "girls."[23] Part of this, of course, can be explained by the fact that in rural areas many young men have not married, nor have they left home to find employment. Those that remained at home, moreover, had relatively little voice in the operation of the family farms. Since there was no national system of primogeniture, a father could keep his sons guessing about who was to inherit the farm, thereby increasing his power.

In sum, authority in Ireland has lodged historically within the older members of the family and the community. Even in present-day Ireland, age constitutes an important focal point for social authority. Deference to males, parents, and the elderly was, of course, more pronounced before World War II. The situation today is changing; indeed, it is changing so fast that some old people are neglected even by their families, and many live in the county homes.[24] For the nation as a whole, however, deference and respect remain a significant component of the Irish political culture.

Social Classes

Despite the authoritarianism that pervades the Irish family system, a seemingly egalitarian theme is found in some of the literature dealing with Irish society—namely, the notion that Ireland has been a classless society since the decline of the Protestant Establishment. The usual reasons given for the lack of class consciousness are the reaction to harsh British rule and to the exploitative, alien upper class of earlier centuries. Irishmen do, indeed, demonstrate few outward manifestations of deference on the basis of class. In private conversation they are openly scornful of upper-class pretenses of superiority, especially if the objects of disrespect happen to be Englishmen. Class is undoubtedly less important in Ireland than in Britain.

Yet Ireland is not really a classless society, for Irish citizens have some rather clear perceptions of class. For example, marriages are heavily influenced by the class backgrounds of the prospective bride or groom. Although opportunities for upward social mobility exist in Ireland, the usual advantages accruing to the upper and middle classes in most societies preclude an absolute equality of opportunity.[25] Also, the evidence clearly indicates that most Irishmen think of themselves as belonging to some class.[26]

On the other hand, compared with societies like Germany and Japan,

Ireland has had far less rigidly stratified classes since independence. In sum, the class system has not been so highly stratified as to militate heavily against the development of a democratic political system.[27]

The Roman Catholic Church

Horace Plunkett, writing in the first decade of the present century, correctly stated that

. . . in no other country in the world, probably, is religion so dominant an element in the daily life of the people as in Ireland, and certainly, nowhere else has the minister of religion so wide and undisputed an authority.[28]

To quote a contemporary analyst more sympathetic to the role of the Catholic church in Ireland:

[The State] is less influential and consistent than the Church, its rank is inferior, not only in the theologian's eyes, but socially. The people put more trust in their bishop than in their deputy. The first represents an older, better established order, steeped in the nation's history.[29]

Examples of the Church's high status in Irish society abound. Although rankings of dignitaries at state functions vary depending upon the occasion and the government department involved, members of the Church hierarchy are invariably accorded high status.[30] Also, as Coogan points out, many important public functions, such as the opening the Dáil, are preceded by mass.[31] At occasions such as wedding receptions, announcements are usually preceded by the phrase: "Reverend Fathers, Ladies and Gentlemen." Moreover, the Constitution of Ireland until December, 1972, posited a ". . . special position of the Holy Catholic Apostolic and Roman Church as the guardian of the Faith professed by the great majority of the citizens."[32]

These examples, however, merely indicate the formal honorary position of the Church. Still more interesting is the actual role of the Church in the day-to-day life of the Irish people. In the last century, the clergy actively engaged in the politics of Ireland under the Union, sometimes in the leadership posts of revolutionary movements and sometimes in prominent positions in the electoral politics of the island. In Limerick, for example, Father Casey was chairman of the United Irish League. The Catholic hierarchy also took positions—often clear and vehement—on important political issues. Thus, the Church denounced the Republican insurgents during the Civil War and the Minister of Health, Noel Browne, resigned in 1951 after the Catholic hierarchy, together with the Irish Medical Association, denounced his mother-and-child, health-care plan. Of course, since independence, open involvement in Irish politics had become less pronounced, especially in such matters as elections. Because of the pervasive social influence of the conservative Church, however, politicians must even today consider possible reactions of the clergy on matters such as education and welfare, even though on most legislation an actual veto power no longer exists.[33]

That Roman Catholicism has infused Irish social life with an authoritarian manner is indicated in countless ways, although it must be remembered that most Irishmen view the Church's role as perfectly legitimate. The Church controls most schools, and runs them in an authoritarian fashion. Despite the rapid modernization of Irish society, even today, especially in rural areas, priests play a major role in the social life of the community. For example, priests take a hand in the production of plays and in the work of cooperatives and credit unions.[34]

The genuine authority of the Church is indicated more sharply by its role in supervising the moral life of the community. People, in their late 20s from one town, reported to the writer that when they had been dating, priests regularly visited the local lovers' lane to send young couples in parked cars on their way. Numerous similar accounts are reported by other writers. Similarly, when an unmarried girl becomes pregnant, the priest often visits the family of the father in order to pressure him into marriage. To be sure, the pervasive involvement and authority of the Catholic clergy is gradually declining, particularly in urban areas, but even in Dublin great deference is shown to priests. And the former Archbishop of Dublin, though not entirely successful, forbad Catholics to attend famed—but characteristically Protestant—Trinity College. Indeed, Arland Ussher, writing decades later than Plunkett, could with some justification, claim that "for the Irish, almost alone among nations today, religion is still the central reality of life, concerning which discussion is unnecessary, if not dangerous."[35] As will be seen in the chapter on secularization, future changes in this area are likely to be slow.

Irish Education

Thus far it has been shown that several of the principal socializing agents in Irish society—namely, the family, the community, and the Roman Catholic church—are strongly authoritarian rather than democratic. It remains to deal with the role of education in Irish society, for the institutions of learning in actual operation often have, as their principle function, inculcation in children of the traditional values of their society.

The most striking feature of the Irish educational system is the fact that it is controlled by organized religion. Ever since the reforms of the nineteenth century, education in Ireland has been dominated by the Church. The managers of the "national" or primary schools are clergymen, either

Catholic or Protestant, indicating, of course, the existence of a separate system of education for Catholic and Protestant children. For reasons suggested in Chapter 2, however, the separate systems of education for Catholics and Protestants, unlike the separate religious schools in Northern Ireland, produce little antipathy between the two religious communities.

In any event, although schools are funded to a large extent by the state, and must meet government standards for physical facilities and curriculum, the system is fundamentally one of private religious education. Furthermore, in a society in which the opinions of Church leaders are accorded serious public and governmental consideration, particularly when the issues under consideration involve social policy, the views of the Church weigh heavily on public officials who shape government standards and regulations.[36]

The style of education in Irish Catholic schools is best described as traditional and authoritarian. Children do not take part in the day-to-day decisions, boys and girls do not usually attend the same schools, and young people do not have the right to regulate their own social activities. Instead, deference to authority, obedience to regulations, and veneration of age and religion are the principal values and themes in Irish education. Frequent and sometimes excessive corporal punishment has been employed, especially in the schools for boys, but, frequently, in the schools for girls as well.[37] Indeed, there has recently been a national debate concerning physical punishment. Because of criticism by intellectuals and some parents, corporal punishment has diminished substantially.

Naturally, most politicians and administrators attended these schools. Indeed S. O. Mathuna points out that the notoriously strict Christian Brothers schools were especially prominent in the training of Irish civil servants, and heavily influenced them.[38] The authoritarianism and inflexibility instilled by this process suggests one possible reason for the desire of the Irish to avoid administrative and organizational channels, and to seek personal intervention by elected representatives.

James S. Coleman is correct when he states that schools do not need civics courses in order to create feelings of loyalty and obedience for the nation and its leaders in students. For example, formal civics training in Britain, as compared with the programs in the United States, is almost non-existent. Coleman also makes the interesting point that mass education need not create democratic values, but, instead, can engender authoritarian values.[39] In any case, even without civics courses, schools can create feelings of loyalty toward the nation because attitudes of deference and obedience may be transferred from one social system to another—in this case, from the schools to the nation and its leaders. Generalized authoritarian values instilled in Irish children by the schools, then, are an indirect but important source of support for the political system.

But the Irish educational process since independence has done much more than this. Through a variety of mechanisms it has attempted the deliberate inculcation of patriotic values. The recent decision to begin formal civics courses reflects the continuing desire to socialize students politically. The Department of Education maintains that "the special object of a course in Civics will be to ensure that the pupils acquire an adequate knowledge of and a proper respect for local and national institutions and of their own rights and responsibilities as citizens."[40] In a more general sense, the Department declares that

. . . the course will have, also, as a prime objective the teaching of the young citizen to recognize and obey lawful authority, to help preserve law, order, and discipline, to respect private and public rights and property and to be ready to defend the national territory should the need arise.[41]

Before the advent of civics courses, schools placed a strong emphasis on the revolutionary struggle against England and on the heroism of leaders of the independence movement, although, as critics noted, there was comparatively little stress on the civil war.[42]

Authoritarian Attitudes

Several key components of authoritarianism in Irish society have been discussed. It was noted, however, that there were qualifications to this authoritarianism: for example, a limited individualism, a flexible attitude toward laws and rules, and a comparatively open class system. Nevertheless, on balance one must conclude that the major structures of Irish society have been quite authoritarian. Even the nature of the democratic political system could be cited as evidence of a strong authoritarian bent. Earlier, it was pointed out that Ireland has one of the most centralized governments of the world's democracies, and there is little evidence that Irish men and women have rebelled against this tendency. Indeed, Francis Litton's conclusions from his, yet unpublished, survey suggested that Dubliners were not especially upset when the Dublin City Council was abolished by the national government.[43] One might also argue that past popular support for Fianna Fáil was, at least partially, the result of stronger central leadership.

Survey data on popular attitudes is, of course, nonexistent for the early years of Irish political development. Yet recent surveys support the argument for the generally authoritarian sentiments of Irish citizens—despite the current secularizing and democratizing trends to be discussed in a later chapter. In a survey of Dubliners conducted in 1966, seventy-one percent of those questioned agreed with the statement that "a few strong leaders would do more for the country than all the laws and talk."[44]

An important, but as yet unpublished, national survey was recently conducted under the supervision of John Raven and C.T. Whelan of the Economic and Social Research Institute of Dublin, and Stein Larsen of The University of Bergen, Bergen, Norway. When published and analyzed in detail, the findings will represent an important addition to the literature on Irish politics, and on comparative politics generally. Among the results of the survey to be briefly noted here are that ninety-three percent of those interviewed felt that "a good strong leader" was important for the future of the country. Indeed, this factor was listed ahead of other alternatives such as "good planning on the part of the government," "the hard work of the people," and "good luck."

Also, with respect to an individual's work situation, the desire for more participation ranked far lower than other factors, such as better facilities. Moreover, the willingness of the public to restrict the political speech of undesirable groups was marked. On the other hand, a certain value conflict was noted with respect to authoritarianism, in that all but thirteen percent questioned felt that ordinary people should have some degree of "greater say" in running the country. This conflict may be partly the result of secularizing trends, to be discussed later, as well as the belief that the only way to get results is to operate through the traditional personalistic structures. Undoubtedly the published analyses of the survey will shed further light on the matter.[45] But as this, and the following chapter make clear, there has been a strong authoritarian tendency in the public's attitude and behavior, and there has been little evidence of an actual tendency toward direct participation.

With respect to the attitudes of leaders, we have seen that their statements have often been quite authoritarian in tone. Reactions to opponents like the IRA and Blueshirts have also been strong. More recently, after the spectacular March, 1973 seizure of arms from a boat off the Irish coast, which were bound for the Provisional IRA, the Minister for Defense with some justification claimed: "This is a law and order nation with a law and order Government."[46]

The Consequences of Authoritarianism

As with traditional values in systems like the Japanese, authoritarian norms in Ireland facilitated the development of an independent Irish nation. Trust, obedience, and deference toward the male head of one's family, toward the elderly, and toward the clergy, predisposed Irishmen to accept the decisions of political authority. Thus, Irishmen at the time of independence were favorably disposed toward the acceptance of national political authority. Of course, British authority was viewed as illegitimate by many Irishmen before independence, but this was because the British were considered foreign exploiters. Moreover, independence movements normally involved only a minority of Irishmen. The 1916 Rising did not have public backing until after the execution of the revolutionaries, and the eventual attempt to impose conscription. At first glance the Civil War may seem a major exception to the acceptance of native rule, but even here the lack of support for the republican forces resulted in part from a popular unwillingness to view elected national rulers as illegitimate.

The resources needed for enforcement were substantially reduced because of public support for the political system and its leaders. With the end of hostilities after the Civil War, the Irish Government could devote more resources to reconstruction and to developmental programs. The reduced need for vigorous enforcement permitted the government to operate in a comparatively mild and democratic manner.[47] It is also possible that authoritarian values, particularly those of a religious nature, reduced demands of political leaders for government goods and services, and thereby reduced the load on the system.

Moreover, the authoritarian Church encouraged support for the new democratic nation. Edward Williams, in discussing Latin American development, said that "the authoritarian patterns of Catholic thought and practice may well furnish the necessary prop for the integrative process through the interim transitional period."[48] He pointed out that the Church helps legitimize developing governments, that the lower levels of the clergy provide linkages between elites and masses, and that peasant organizations help provide ideological justification for social change.[49] In the case of Ireland, it is clear that the Church did all three, although the latter two roles were especially crucial during the nineteenth century.

A crucial consequence of authoritarian norms in Ireland has been the support provided for the development and maintenance of organizations. This consideration is of importance not only because of the need in developing nations to create effective and flexible agencies in government, but also because of the need to establish economic organizations capable of sustaining long-term economic growth. Hence, the present chapter will conclude by discussing the implications of authoritarian social norms for the establishment of effective organizations in Ireland.

As Edward Banfield observed, individuals in organizations must possess the capacity to accept and carry out orders, if their organization is to survive or operate in an efficient manner.[50] At the least, there must be a substantial willingness on the part of workers to accept day-to-day supervision and to accept basic organizational guidelines. For, despite present trends toward greater democratization, the principal means of achieving coordination remain hierarchical for most organizations. Furthermore, many organizational tasks are sometimes best handled by hierarchically-structured administrative units. Because the administrative needs of any nation require the accomplishment of substantial amounts of work of this type, developing nations must employ hierarchical organizations. To be sure, flexibility is sometimes best achieved through non-hierarchical, group-centered forms. Even where innovation is required, however, hierarchical administration, especially where there is built-in competition among administrative units, can stimulate initiative and innovation.

Additionally, authoritarian norms help create loyalty toward the organization. There must be some commitment among members to the preservation of the organization and to the enhancement of its goals. Even when organizations are established to achieve short-term goals, there must be a willingness to work toward the achievement of those goals, and a desire to preserve the organization as a means of accomplishing them.

It is clear, in short, that authoritarianism stimulates loyalty and a willingness on the part of the employees to accept direction. It is not, of course, maintained that authoritarian values are the only means of developing effective organizations. But, in developing nations, one often finds sentiments that are detrimental to administrative development. Often people are unable to get along with others in the organization, and are unwilling to accept supervision or to work toward the achievement of administrative goals. More universal are feelings of alienation, uncertainty, and hostility brought about by rapid social change and by the decline in traditional values. Clearly, then, authoritarian social beliefs are a principal source of positive associational sentiments and administrative loyalty.

Authoritarian values, of course, have a number of negative organizational implications. From a democratic perspective, they can reduce opportunities for self-fulfillment. They can stifle initiative, increase commitment to formal routine, at the expense of organizational goals, and lead to unsympathetic treatment of clients. Furthermore, authoritarianism, can lead to excessive administrative centralization that may breed inefficiencies. There is clearly a place for regional planning and other decentralizing mechanisms.[51] However, these administrative techniques are not inconsistent with the political culture. But, if one assumes widespread political participation by the public in a more decentralized system, he is likely to find a lack of popular responsiveness and probable domination of decentralized political structure by local elites.

In sum, authoritarianism has, in the Irish context, been a beneficial component of the political culture. Democratic political procedures and institutions had been viewed as legitimate before independence. Authoritarian sentiments helped reinforce their legitimacy after the new state was founded. Furthermore, while authoritarian norms increased support for organizations and produced a willingness to accept some regulation, personalism, as we shall see, has provided a mechanism for circumventing the arbitrariness and inflexibility that often accompany authoritarian institutions. Moreover, Irish resistance to regimentation, and ambivalence toward laws and regulations, constituted another built-in check upon extreme authoritarianism and organizational rigidity. Authoritarianism in Ireland, then, helped support administrative and democratic political development.

5 Irish Personalism

Virtually every writer about Irish society has observed the importance of close personal connections among community and family members. While all societies maintain important networks of interpersonal organization, few have been so pronounced as the Irish pattern, and many have been far less cohesive. Writing in 1972, T. A. Callanan was probably correct in arguing that ". . . the personal dimension is still stronger in this country [Ireland] than in any other."[1]

Personalism refers to a pattern of social relations in which people are valued for who they are and whom they know—not solely for what technical qualifications they possess. Where extreme personalism exists, family and friends determine one's chances for success. The ability to obtain a good job depends upon connection to the right family or clique. The capacity to win a government contract depends not on submission of the lowest bid, but on having the "right" associations. Even the treatment received from police, or the sentence given by a judge, depends on these personal considerations. In politics, the public interest means the interests of the leader and his followers, together with their families and friends. The public treasury becomes a private preserve for whoever controls government. This kind of personalism, of course, exists in ascriptive societies.

There is a burgeoning literature about patron-client relations. Writings by John Duncan Powell, Lemarchand, Legg, Scott, Kaufman, and others, emphasize the applicability of the concept of clientelism in the analysis of such societies as Latin America.[2] Though one might usefully employ clientelism in the analysis of Irish Politics, there is a nearly universal tendency for writers in this field to note a strongly inequalitarian quality to such relations. Interactions normally take place between superiors or patrons and subordinates to whom favors are dispensed. Yet, as we shall see, this patron-dimension has not really been central to Irish politics since peasant times. Rather, the Irish pattern is one of brokerage and reciprocal favors—often among equals. However imperfect from the standpoint of participative norms, often regarded as important for "civic cultures," Irish personalism, as it has existed in independent Ireland, has been a mechanism for public control of politicians.[3]

One could also make a good case for employing the pattern variables of Talcott Parsons; this work has, of course, benefited from the Parsonian analyses.[4] Yet there is great overlap in these variables, and the rigorous utilization of such concepts as diffuseness, ascription, universalism, particularism, etc., would unnecessarily complicate and obfuscate the analysis. It will become clear within the writer's terminology, for instance, that achievement criteria are often employed in a particularistic pattern in Ireland. Finally, and most importantly, the writer does not wish to obscure by terminology an important normative dimension of the discussion for modern societies in general, and Ireland in particular—namely, the psychological and political implications of personal style, as well as the trend toward depersonalization that often accompanies economic and technological modernization. Hence, the term "personalism" is considered especially appropriate for the present study.

Personalism, then, can exist in societies in which achievement is more important than ascribed characteristics. In such cases, standards of evaluation based on achievement are applied in a personal manner. If an individual meets the basic qualifications for a job, as might several other applicants, he may receive the job on the basis of personal characteristics, such as his family connections. In other words, achievement standards can be applied in a highly personal manner.

Universalism, however, is more characteristic of modern societies. Here procedures, rules, and laws tend to be followed, regardless of personal considerations. Universalism is therefore a bureaucratic phenomenon. To obtain a good job one must meet educational requirements and achieve more than other applicants in the entrance examinations. To start a business one must meet licensing regulations, regardless of one's family and friendship ties. To be promoted, one need only perform better than one's peers.

Personalism and universalism are matters of degree. Both exist in all societies. Even modern bureaucratic nations have important personalistic features. Students of public administration have long known that informal organizations enable administrative agencies to operate effectively. Administrators who want to accomplish a particular task sometimes must ignore the organization's chain of command and turn to someone outside it who can accomplish the job. Similarly, rules sometimes must be broken in order to achieve administrative goals. Nevertheless, social and economic modernization normally accentuates universal norms, and leads to a radical decline in personalism.

Universalism encourages administrators to treat persons objectively, rather than as individual human beings. This has contributed to the alienation of young people, and others who want, at least, some consideration as individual personalities, even though they may accept achievement and, even, universal standards. The discontent generated by depersonalization is not new. Nor is it limited to a particular sector of the social or political spectrum. For decades American conservatives have criticized national bureaucracies for stifling personal initiative and for failing to recognize the need for flexibility is encouraging economic growth. Liberals, on the other hand, criticized bureaucracies for their inhumane treatment of clients—for example, black welfare recipients. The current clamor of youth in modern nations against depersonalization is the culmination of a long period of growing discontent. Therefore, an analysis of personalism in Ireland may prove useful, not only to students of political development in Ireland and the developing areas of the world, but also to students of modern political systems.

Personalism in Irish Society

In Chapters 2 and 3 it was shown that Ireland effectively withstood the pressures and strains of modernization, and successfully established viable democratic institutions. It is therefore apparent that the social and cultural environment was not sufficiently hostile to result in the breakdown of the political system. On the contrary, Ireland possessed highly cohesive social and cultural systems that supported democratic development. There was little of the hostility and distrust that have plagued other developing nations.

The clannish quality of life in early Celtic society pervades the historical literature.[5] While this trait characterized many early societies, it was particularly pronounced in Ireland. The existence of small rural communities and the absence of large cities facilitated its perpetuation. The small size of the country and its population also contributed to the continuation of a personalistic style, because personal ties were less likely to be broken by geographic mobility, and because a comparatively large percentage of citizens could be personally known to one another. Most shops and factories, moreover, remained small, and therefore increased the importance of personalism in these organizations.[6]

At the time of independence, personalism was quite pronounced. Everything was influenced by one's connections. Many jobs were obtained through personal intermediaries. Promotions depended as much upon personal connections as upon performance. The predominant social value was loyalty to family and friends.

It is fortunate that the emphasis on Irish culture and politics, during the first part of the century, resulted in a number of discerning works. One of the most perceptive writers was the French scholar Paul-DuBois, who argued that a strong sense of community was one of the central characteristics of the Irish mentality. Discussing the importance of group ties, Paul-DuBois maintained that " . . . no one is more dominated by the social instinct, the need for society, than the Celt of Ireland. The Englishman does not fear solitude; the Irishman loves company and needs contact with his kind."[7]

Horace Plunkett, who was hostile to some features of Irish culture and society, such as the central role of the Roman Catholic church, advocated cooperativism as the best method of regenerating Irish society and fostering economic development. He believed that the Irishman's strong sense of group identity could serve as a useful foundation for the development of an economically successful cooperative movement that would have the additional advantage of democratizing Irish society. He was, therefore, one of the earliest writers to recognize the significance of Irish associational norms for the development of effective organizations.[8] To be sure, Plunkett lamented what he felt to be a lack of initiative and industry in the Irish character, but he perceived clearly that social cohesion is a major building block of effective organizations. Whatever else he thought of his countrymen, he knew that they trusted each other enough to work well together, given sufficient motivation. Although his cooperative movement achieved only modest long-term success, his views on the inherent cooperativeness of Irishmen were proved correct by subsequent Irish history.

Much later in the century, Arensberg's and Kimball's important study of Irish social organization in County Clare was carried out. The book described a society replete with mutual support based upon personal considerations. For example, farmers assisted one another at harvests, and lived by a system of reciprocal obligations which permeated the entire community. Although patterns of mutual support could be found in other nations, few were so pronounced as those of the Irish. Moreover, unlike the hostile interpersonal relations in other countries, described earlier, social relations in Clare, and throughout Ireland, were usually based on mutual trust and assistance.[9]

Of course, Eileen Kane's work suggests that obligations among kin were not limitless.[10] Moreover, as Hannan has demonstrated, there are various kinds of personalistic networks. He notes that, partly because of the location of their study, Arensberg and Kimball did not adequately deal with such common networks as neighborhood patterns. Far more than the kinship networks described by Arensberg and Kimball, these neighborhood networks are based more upon reciprocal assistance. Unlike kinship patterns, people in these systems have little right to expect support unless they are prepared to repay at a later stage. In times of a death in the family, neighbors naturally help out, but continuing aid after the initial emergency is expected to come from relatives. Moreover, social cohesiveness was never perfect. Rivalries often existed, people sometimes reneged on favors granted, and there was a propensity not to assist someone if it resulted in elevation of his social or economic status above one's own.[11] We shall also note, shortly, other negative consequences of Irish personalism. Nonetheless, comparatively speaking, Irish rural society was quite cohesive and mutually supportive.

Many personalistic traits had their roots in Irish family organization. The Irish nuclear family was one of the tightest and most cohesive social organizations to be found anywhere. Loyalty to one's parents, especially in the first half of the century, was one of the most important social values. Children were considered to be a great blessing. Despite male dominance, girls as well as boys were highly valued.

The most remarkable feature of the Irish family to the outside observer is the cohesiveness and expansiveness of the extended family. In Ireland the saying "blood is thicker than water" describes a central reality of the society. Even distant relatives often have a claim on their families for assistance and support. There is no more effective means of accomplishing a task than by having a well-placed relative. In earlier rural Irish society, this could mean anything from borrowing a plow to applying for government services. It is still true that having a relative in a position of influence greatly increases one's chances for success in almost any area of life. In the public bureaucracy this principle operates mainly on an other-things-being-equal basis, because there is little outright corruption in government. But, because government today interacts with so many people, other things are often nearly equal. Also, if one comes close to the necessary legal qualifications, one will get the benefit of the doubt. Furthermore, red tape is cut quickly when one's cousin is a civil servant in the appropriate agency.[12] In the private sector the power of relatives extends much further—from obtaining reduced prices on commercial products to winning a position from among a hundred qualified applicants.

Irish personalism is not limited to relatives. The next best source of assistance is a friend, or a "friend of a friend." While ties of friendship are important in all societies, in Ireland they become a paramount feature of life. People think first of whom they know, even in the most routine circumstances. Even when dealing with modern, technologically sophisticated organizations, the style is characteristically personal.

Economic development and urbanization have not eradicated personalism in Ireland. Although Humphreys, for example, notes the increasing importance of modern organizations, such as factories, and acknowledges the declining role of the family, he points out that neighborhood social organizations remain supportive rather than hostile, and sees ". . . a radical continuity between the general pattern of the family in Dublin and the rural community. . . ."[13] Interaction with relatives continues, and loyalty toward the family remains a principal value, despite the growing importance of other socializing forces such as peer groups. In short, "cross-culturally, the urban family and familial kinship and neighborhood groupings in Dublin are undoubtedly among the very strongest in solidarity and power to be found in urban communities in Western societies."[14]

Yet this social cohesiveness also has negative consequences. Personal privacy is almost impossible. Everyone knows everyone's business, especially in rural communities. Nor, as has been indicated, are Irishmen always charitable and neighborly. In his polemical novel, *The Valley of the Squinting Windows,* Brinsley MacNamara portrays a society governed by insidious gossip. Old women destroy lives by taking it upon themselves to interfere with the affairs of neighbors. In one instance, letters which could have led to a marriage are intercepted. Even priests join in the destruction of reputations. Of course,

MacNamara exaggerates, but he does caution us against drawing a one-sided picture of Irish social life.[15] More recently Connery has said that "What the Irish seem to like least about themselves is their habit of belittling and backbiting."[16] However, mutual trust and support are quite strong.

Personalism in Irish Politics

Elected representatives in all democratic nations run errands for constituents, but in Ireland this function is especially pronounced. Electoral districts are small. Unlike many English MP's, Irish legislators live among their constituents. As Cohan puts it, ". . . people in any given constituency want a local man to represent them in the Dáil."[17] Unlike American congressmen and senators, Irish representatives have little role in the formulation of legislation and can devote more time to doing personal favors. The proportional representation system, moreover, places representatives in competition with other legislators in their districts.

Above all, it is the cultural style of Irish citizens to operate through intermediaries, and it helps to know these intermediaries personally. Although deputies intercede for any of their constituents, it is normally more effective to know the legislator personally or to communicate with him through a relative or a friend who knows him personally. In most other democratic nations it is far more common to approach legislators directly.[18]

Bax points out, moreover, that there exists a highly developed brokerage system in Irish politics, involving not only TD's and local councillors, but various other political intermediaries such as members of local party clubs. Most of the demands placed on politicians involve interceding on behalf of constituents in routine cases of administration. When administrators are especially accommodating they may receive help from politicians in such matters as promotions. In sum, Irish politicians are not patrons as such, because they do not directly grant favors. Rather, they tend to act as brokers between citizens and those administrators who actually control the resources.[19] Though more negative than the present writer, Bax does suggest that the brokerage system is deeply rooted in the political culture and probably could not be easily changed, except at great risk to the system.

Personal considerations, moreover, greatly affect one's chances of winning elections in Ireland. Widows and sons of representatives who died in office are usually almost certain to win the elections called to fill the seats.[20] As Basil Chubb points out:

The last five by-elections before the 1965 general election saw the return of three widows and one son. Of these four relatives, three held their seats at the general election and one did not stand. This strengthens an already strong dynastic element in Irish politics.[21]

In a study of the 1969 elections in a County Donegal constituency, Paul Sacks also stressed the importance of personal considerations in that contest, maintaining that "a part of the character of localism in Donegal is the high value placed on personal contact in politics."[22] He went on to stress the importance of personal contacts in dealing with the administrative branch of government.[23]

Few avenues to political office surpass fame in hurling or other Gaelic sports; indeed, this particular phenomenon is increasing.[24] Additionally, the former success of independent deputies further illustrates the importance of personalism in Irish politics. These independent deputies, moreover, played a role of greater significance than their numbers would appear to suggest, because they sometimes possessed enough swing votes to control the balance of power in the Dáil. Frequently, however, independents have voted consistently with one of the major parties, thereby preserving the stability of parliamentary government. The number since independence varied between twelve and twenty-four, a significant figure in view of the Dáil's small size. A substantial share of the independents' success was attributable, of course, to proportional representation, because multi-member constituencies aid parties and candidates lacking plurality support. But, even more important is the consideration that Irish voters give to personal attributes. Although independents did better at the local community level,

. . . in Dublin there have often been one or more such members, whose position has been entirely based on "citizen's advice" type of service and on success in obtaining public housing and other benefits. For this reason, also, some deputies who have broken with their parties have nevertheless retained their seats.[25]

Since independents, even more than party-affiliated deputies, depended on errand running in order to win electoral support, their presence in Irish politics increased the level of personalism in the political process even more.

The personalistic character of Irish politics is also reflected by advancement practices within the political parties. It has been standard procedure for sons of leaders who fought in the war of independence to receive ministerial posts. Personal connections of this sort weigh more heavily than parliamentary experience in determining one's prospects for political success within the parties. Party leadership is, therefore, something of a family tradition.[26]

A significant manifestation of Irish personalism is the manner in which citizens engage in politics. Implicit in the discussion of the role of deputies was the argument that citizens prefer personal channels. Survey evidence supports that contention. Ian Hart's analysis of a 1967 survey of Dublin voters shows that "Dubliners were not very aware of the possibilities of informal group action."[27] When asked how they would try to influence their local government, only fifteen percent said that they would organize an informal group, or arouse friends and neighbors in a letter-writing or petition campaign.[28]

More recently, the ESRI public opinion project, supervised by Larsen, Raven, and Whelan revealed similar tendencies. In response to an open-ended question about what one would do to oppose an unjust law passed by the Dáil, fifty-two percent of subjective competents (people who felt their action could be effective) mentioned contacting a TD; only four percent suggested protesting through an organized group. Similarly, for local laws viewed as unjust, forty-two percent suggested contacting local elected representatives, and twelve percent mentioned contacting their TD. Again the proposed use of organized groups was limited: it was suggested by only five percent.[29]

Furthermore, this and other data in the survey suggest that the percentage of the total electorate which would work through informal groups was quite low, compared with most Western democracies. This survey project dealt, of course, with issues other than those noted here, and the published versions of it will include comparative data and details not discussed above. For present purposes, however, the point is that the findings of this important survey project further document the pronounced tendency of the Irish toward a personalistic approach to politics.

Consequences of Personalism

Personalism in Ireland has provided a workable alternative to the more strongly institutionalized arrangements to be found in other democratic nations. It has not bred great corruption. It is the reflection of a cohesive social system that emphasizes family and friendship, and that generates inter-personal trust. It may be said, therefore, that it surely contributed to the social integration that was necessary for the political development of the new Irish nation.

Because depersonalization in modern nations is a principal cause of discontent, the retention of a personalistic style in Ireland moderates the dissatisfactions generated by the rapidly accelerating modernization. For, although Ireland is fast becoming an organizational society, it has managed to retain a significant degree of personalism in human relations. This is particularly important because the Irish intensely dislike bureaucratic procedures, and they abhor regimentation.

Yet Irish personalism, like many political phenomena, has harmful as well as helpful consequences. It is often unfair. If a man happens to have more influential associations than do others, he can derive more benefits from the system. This, of course, runs counter to the political and administrative ideal that persons in like circumstances ought to be treated alike. In a more practical vein, personalism also produces discontent. A qualified applicant for a job, who loses the position to a third cousin of the company vice-president, is not likely to support the system at that particular time. Moreover, if youth and dissidents lose access to personal channels within the political system, the future stability of Ireland will be jeopardized. This is a real danger, because of the conservative and authoritarian character of the Irish political culture. At present, however, most Irishmen accept the personalistic nature of the system, even if they sometimes lose. This is in no small measure a result of the fact that universalistic criteria are combined with personal considerations. The boss's third cousin is often well qualified. Furthermore, the person who is unfairly excluded from the benefits of personalism typically reacts, not by attacking the system, but by seeking new personalistic channels—he goes out looking for a third cousin of his own.

Personalism also produces inefficiencies. The vast amounts of time that Irish legislators spend running errands leaves them with time for little else. They have comparatively little responsibility for formulating policy. Also, as we saw in Chapter 2, there is little legislative oversight of bureaucratic policy making.

Economic development suffers to the extent that personalism diminishes the degree of universalism in recruitment practices. Fortunately for Ireland, the more blatant kinds of abuse found in most developing nations seldom have occurred, because people normally have had to meet at least minimal requirements. Nevertheless, personalism in both recruitment and promotion practices impedes efficiency and slows economic growth.

But the immediate problem of new nations is national integration, and there is nothing more fundamental to this process than a political culture that generates social, political, and organizational cohesion, rather than fragmentation. This is far more important, initially, than economic development. Indeed, economic growth is often destabilizing in the short run because it increases the rate of modernization, and because distribution of new wealth is seldom equitable. For this reason the marginal benefits lost to a slower economic growth are far less significant than the benefits derived from a supportive political culture.

Moreover, personalism facilitated the development of adaptable, efficient administrative agencies, in that it helped produce viable informal organizations. Irish personalism tends to be supportive rather than hostile, with the result that flexibility and effective channels of communications have been more easily fostered. No organization can operate effectively solely on the basis of formal rules and structures, and it helps to have administrators willing to ignore occasionally official guidelines. In short, Irish personalism aided the growth of comparatively effective public and private organizations and was a principal means of escaping the bureaucratic rigidity which a highly authoritarian political culture might otherwise have produced. As McCarthy, the Devlin Report, and other sources have pointed out, Irish administration is by no means perfect. But, compared with other nations, both developing and modern, it has been rather successful.[30]

Therefore, personalism has been a quite fortunate component of the Irish political culture. It has given Ireland a solid base on which to construct a viable democratic policy. Yet, the Irish Republic has long since passed the crucial early years of political development. Now the challenges of social modernization and economic development are more crucial. Some decline in the more negative features of personalism is inevitable as Ireland continues to modernize. Technical qualifications will undoubtedly become more important, as economic development continues. The problem is to sustain greater universalism without sacrificing the benefits of a personal style. The past persistence of traditional norms suggests that this problem can be surmounted.

6 Secularization and the Impact of the Northern Ireland Crisis

It is ironic that two such seemingly undemocratic traits as personalism and authoritarianism should have been such an important force in supporting the democratic political development of the Irish political system. Yet what may be helpful at one stage of development may be harmful at later stages, if the previous values and structures fail to adapt to social, economic, and political change.[1] Furthermore, what may be supportive for internal political development can have negative consequences for wider political settings. After all, the southern Irish state has survived for more than fifty years, and its very existence has had a profound impact on politics in Northern Ireland. Northern Ireland, in turn, has played an important role in the politics of the Republic, particularly since 1968. Hence, we shall now deal more explicitly with cultural change and briefly consider North-South relations from the standpoint of political culture and democratic political development.

The concept of "secularization" will provide a convenient basis for our discussion of cultural change. Many scholars see secularization as vital to the process of political development. Indeed, Donald Smith has argued that since the early nineteenth century ". . . *the secularization of the polity has been the most fundamental structural and ideological change in the process of political development.*"[2] According to Smith, this process includes the separation of the polity from religious institutions, the expansion of government in socio-economic regulations, such as control of welfare and education, the transvaluation of the political culture from transcendent to temporal polity-dominated values, and, sometimes, the dominance of the polity over religious structures and beliefs.[3] Gabriel Almond and G. Bingham Powell have also specified secularization as one of the central components of political development. They define secularization as ". . . the process whereby men become increasingly rational, analytical, and empirical in their political action." Their definition emphasizes cultural rather than structural aspects of the phenomenon, and they maintain that in addition to pragmatic, empirical orientations, there is also a change from diffuse to specific orientations.[4]

Sources of Change

Of course, as we have already seen, the new Irish state was substantially secularized from the start. Church and state were formally and substantially separate; there has been little overt persecution of minority religions. And, from the beginning, Irish governments have taken a substantially pragmatic and interventionist approach toward the role of government in society and the economy. To be sure, education, censorship, and other areas discussed earlier, did suggest some important overlapping, as did the more subtle forms of intervention noted in Chapters 2 and 4. Moreover, reflecting Catholic ideals, divorce is prohibited by the constitution, and birth control items may not be sold legally. On the whole, however, structural secularization involving church and state was sufficient to place Ireland in the democratic category.

A lesser degree of secularization was to be found in the minds and hearts of Irish citizens, and only recently has the transvaluation of the political culture made significant advances. As Hugh Brody and others have demonstrated, the communal, authoritarian, and personalistic structures in rural Ireland have undergone a profound decline. The need for reciprocal support has largely vanished with mechanization, reliance upon a money economy, welfare measures, and other changes.[5]

Moreover, the value accorded a rural way of life has dwindled radically. The decline in interdependence has helped produce a decline in close social interactions. In rural communities today, people are less likely to know their neighbors or to interact with them. "The erosion of mutual aid has made way for an ethic of independence."[6] But the demoralization of rural Ireland is by no means complete. It depends upon the geographic area, and there are limited counter trends, such as festivals and other signs of revival.

It is strikingly apparent that young people, in rural as well as urban areas, seek to be modern and value the styles and institutions emanating from Dublin and other urban settings, such as London. With so many of the young migrating to cities, and with others turning to them for their standard of values, traditional authority structures break down. Farmers no longer retain a strong hold over sons who have little desire to inherit and work the family farm or to remain on the land. Government officials are more likely than ever to make important decisions affecting communities, rather than are groups of local, elderly men. Also, Ireland is fast becoming an urban society. In short, both authoritarian and personalistic structures have weakened significantly since the 1950s.

Similarly, the role of the Church has undergone dramatic changes. The spirit of ecumenism has penetrated the Church and schools. Joint religious services, an increasing dialogue among various religious bodies, and a new trend toward emphasizing tolerance in schools are manifestations of this development. Nor is this trend solely a response to the conflict in Northern Ireland. Church officials and teachers reported to the writer in 1967 that the new ecumenical spirit emanating from Rome modified the attitudes of the Church hierarchy, clerics, and educators. Comparatively few Catholic children in the Republic today are likely to believe that the devil resides in

Protestant churches. The growing tolerance is, unfortunately, marred by the conflict in the North. Nevertheless, Protestantism as such is probably seldom seen as the source of the problem, even by unsophisticated children.

It would be naive, of course, to assume that old prejudices on either side have vanished. They have not. But, compared with earlier periods, there is a distinct and growing willingness to accord respect and a degree of veracity to the beliefs of others. The Catholic church, then, is less absolute as an authority structure, both in terms of its actions as well as in the attitudes of Irish citizens.

Furthermore, the influence of the Church in government inevitably declines as economic and technological modernization proceeds. Although, as John Whyte shows, Church intervention in politics has varied both in intensity and with respect to decision area, there is little doubt that the overall trend is toward less influence.[7] All modern governments tend to become increasingly total in scope. Growing intervention in the economy and other areas places an enormous administrative burden on political systems. Even parliamentarians in democratic nations are steadily losing power to bureaucrats, who have the facilities for handling the complex and technologically-sophisticated burdens of administering a modern nation state.

Even if they were so inclined, clerics could scarcely keep abreast of all important areas of government. This limitation certainly does not mean that the Church will lose interest or influence in all policy matters. The recent conflict over community schools, concerned in part with clerical versus secular control, suggests that such areas as education, and other issues such as family planning, will continue to be heavily influenced not only by the Church itself, but also by an Irish public that still clings to many sacred norms. The failure of efforts in 1972 to liberalize laws and regulations on contraception illustrates the resistance of old structures and values to change.

But, the entire culture of Irish society is being transformed by the impact of social and economic modernization. The increasing percentage of people living in cities, for example, exposes more citizens to a less personalistic and authoritarian environment. It certainly weakens social controls over the young, who have the advantage of greater anonymity in an urban setting. For good or ill, bigness helps liberate people from tight traditional controls.

The impact of movies, television, books, and magazines confronts citizens, especially the young, with ideas and values radically different from the conservatism of traditional Irish society. Returning emigrants often serve a similar function.[8] Moreover, entry into the Common Market will surely expose the Irish to more cosmopolitan values. Not the least of the European Community's impact will be a still greater stress upon material as opposed to sacred values. Some of the fatalism so characteristic of earlier Irish society was the product of a profound lack of opportunity for upward social and economic mobility, even though this fatalism was strongly reinforced by the Church. Today, with greater opportunities for advancement and with the demonstration of comparative economic well-being in urban areas and in much of Europe, few of the young are disposed to placidly accept economic poverty or a quiet, conservative social life.

The greater emphasis upon materialism and liberalization of sexual and social codes, weakens the grasp of family and Church on the young. In societies undergoing rapid technological and social change, the young become the promoters of new trends and fashions, and peer groups increasingly set the tone and standards of social life. The elderly cannot keep up with such rapid change. However much this trend may be resented in Ireland, some of the elite accept it with little resistance. Probably in relatively few areas today would priests feel free to walk down local lovers' lanes attempting to enforce their moral standards on the young, and a growing number of the clergy would themselves willingly reject this kind of role.

Indeed, in Ireland, as elsewhere, there is an increasing tendency for religious leaders, including the Catholic hierarchy, to take on materialistic goals. In a sense, then, religion itself is becoming secularized. The growing concern for the plight of the poor, and the need for government action in social welfare illustrates the point. One could even argue that secularization may be a means of revitalizing religion.

Despite the virtually worldwide displacement of transcendental by secular values, and the frequent tendency to view this trend as a component of modernization, there is little evidence for assuming that human beings do not need religious values or their functional equivalents—such as extreme nationalism. The alienation and sense of purposelessness often characteristic of modern man may be a partial result of secularization. Thus, extreme secularization could lead, not to greater political development, but to political decay. Further, a decline in the authority of the Church as one of the principal legitimizers of Irish government may weaken support for the political system in times of stress, or when major political changes are required. Thus, the modernization and revitalization of Catholicism, from the standpoint of continuing political development, could be a fortunate alternative to the demise of religion.

Relations with Northern Ireland

One of the consequences of the Irish quest for Home Rule, and of the Anglo-Irish War, was the partitioning of Ireland. Northern Protestants were for the most part fanatically opposed to Home Rule, where, in an all-Ireland parliament, they would have been greatly outnumbered by Catholics. As the result of a complex series of events and causes, Ireland was partitioned; six counties in the North were given their own parliament in 1920, while remaining a part of the United Kingdom.[9] As we saw earlier, the remaining twenty-six counties eventually won virtually complete independence.

The new six-county state, established mainly to accommodate northern Protestants, made Protestants a permanent majority. That state has undergone neither democratic political development, nor political development generally. The political system failed to institutionalize structures and processes capable of meeting the needs and demands of all its citizens—a failing that became increasingly apparent under the economic and social modernization of the 1960s. The core of the problem has been the existence of two distinct (though not necessarily unified) communities, identifiable broadly as Catholic on the one hand, and Protestant on the other. Today Catholics constitute roughly thirty-five percent of the population, with Protestants representing the bulk of the remainder.[10]

The conflict is not over religion, as such. Hostilities are rooted in centuries of struggle emanating largely from the seventeenth-century plantations and settlements of Scottish and English Protestants at the expense of native Gaelic Catholics.[11] Naturally polarization was never complete; many leaders of Irish nationalist movements have been Protestants, and northern Presbyterians, and others occasionally united with the Catholics. But a number of historical events, including the Union of 1801, Catholic emancipation, and, especially, the introduction of Home Rule Bills in London in the late nineteenth and early twentieth centuries, created intense differences between the two communities. In Belfast, where hostilities have been particularly intense, sectarian rioting has flared up throughout the nineteenth and twentieth centuries.[12]

There are several key dimensions of this complex problem. One is international: the northern minority views itself as Irish, and, particularly among the working classes, there is, among many, strong sentiment in favor of unification. Moreover, the imposition of internment without trial in 1971, as a security measure, was directed almost entirely against Catholics, and helped solidify Catholics of all economic levels against the system.

The Protestant community, on the other hand, is united in its rejection of a united Ireland, wherein they would form a distinct minority. They have favored the link with Britain, combined with a strong local parliament. Though extremist Protestant ideology greatly overstates the case, there is a certain rationality to Protestant fears. Not only does the constitution of the Republic claim sovereignty over Northern Ireland,[13] but also there are several important components of Catholic doctrine found in southern law; e.g., the prohibition of divorce and of the sale of contraceptive devices, among others.[14] Above all, many Protestants hold an exaggerated notion of the political role of the Catholic church, and reject the authoritarian overtones of the southern political culture. In any event they do not want to give up their privileged position.

Another dimension of the problem concerns the internal politics of Northern Ireland. Since 1920, the Protestant Unionist party has dominated the internal politics of Northern Ireland. Partly because of the concentration of power in the parliamentary system of the Northern Irish government, the minority could be virtually ignored. From the Protestant perspective, the Catholic community has, on the whole, been a disloyal lot that neither deserved nor could safely be given a significant role in government. The Irish nationalist sentiments of many northern Catholics have made them potential traitors in the eyes of the Protestant community. Much of the repression and discrimination against Catholics in the North resulted from an often fanatic fear of "Rome Rule" should the border vanish, as well as a more pragmatic awareness of the self-serving advantages of discrimination. As numerous commentators have noted, there thus exist two minorities, each with rather understandable concerns about cultural and national identity: an actual minority of Roman Catholics in the North, many of whom hold Irish nationalist sentiments, and a potential minority of Protestants who would be greatly outnumbered by Catholics in an all-Ireland nation.

In short, historically there has been little repression of Protestants in the Republic. But there has been substantial repression of Catholics in the North, not in terms of their ability to practice their faith, but rather in terms of political and economic equality.[15] It was these inequalities that spawned the Civil Rights Movement of the 1960s, and, ultimately, led to the present violence.

Because so much of the Protestant attitude has been based on fear of religious persecution in a United Ireland, there has been pressure on the Republic's government to further secularize its political institutions and processes. A symbolic manifestation of this was the ending by referendum in 1972 of the clause giving a "special position" to the Catholic church in the Republic's constitution. The clause, of course, gave the Church no real powers. It is also possible that laws concerning contraception will be liberalized and that, even though divorce will probably not be permitted in the Republic, some kinds of guarantees may be given northern Protestants, covering such matters in Northern Ireland, should unification ultimately take place. It is likely, also, that the Ulster crisis will hasten the trend toward ecumenism within the Republic.

The British White Paper, released in March 1973, provides for a Conference to be held between representatives of the Republic and Northern Ireland, as a prelude to the establishment of a Council of Ireland, which would presumably have quite limited powers concerning common interests in such matters as economics.[16] Few in North or South want immediate unification. Such a move would almost surely lead to a full-scale civil war in the North between the two northern communities, where even now roughly 17,000 British soldiers are unable to maintain order. Indeed, British forces have become part of the problem and are fiercely hated by large sectors of the Catholic community. Yet, many favoring ultimate unification, including members of the Republic's government, see the need for the presence of the British until peace is restored. Sophisticated politicians realize that the task of governing a culturally-fragmented community would be an enormous undertaking, even under a federal arrangement. There is, also, little evidence that the Republic's citizens strongly favor unification.[17]

Nevertheless, from the standpoint of Church involvement in the politics of the Republic, as well as the Catholic content of public policy, the struggle in Northern Ireland has probably hastened the pace of secularization. But the overall impact of the northern turmoil has not been exclusively one of liberalization. A principal aspect of the international dimension of the conflict has been the use of the Republic as a sanctuary by members of the Irish Republican Army engaged in the struggle against the military and civil authorities in the North. Ultimately, in late 1972, this resulted in the suspension of certain civil liberties in the Republic in order to more effectively deal with the Provisional IRA and its political wing, the Provisional Sinn Féin party. Briefly, the provisions included, among other things, special non-jury courts, the admissibility of hearsay evidence, and the assumption of guilt until innocence is proven.[18] Moreover, as the spectacular arms trials of 1970 indicate, top level cabinet members were implicated in the delivery of weapons to the IRA in the North.[19] The exact degree of government involvement is still uncertain.

The impact of limited secularization in the Republic upon Northern Ireland politics is, thus far, quite small. It will certainly not change the immediate goals of Protestant loyalists, for the core issues involve ethnic and national identities, as well as the question of who is to dominate the system.[20] Religion as such represents only a small part of the problem.

Clearly, the government in Northern Ireland has been radically secularized by the suspension of the Northern Irish parliament and by the imposition of direct British rule in March 1972. The new assembly to be established under the White Paper will have, if successfully instituted, only limited authority initially, and ultimate authority will remain in the hands of the United Kingdom government for the foreseeable future. Though the political and economic systems of Northern Ireland still favor the Protestant community, the thrust of British efforts aim at democratization of the system. Their limited success thus far results from a variety of factors, including the inherent difficulties in ending discrimination, the intransigence of extremists on both sides, the breakdown of civil control and their own sometimes belated and mishandled policies. There is little evidence, however, that U.K. officials are bigoted toward Catholics per se. It is probably closer to the truth to say that the British authorities now have a disdain, and sometimes contempt, for both sides. Northern Ireland's membership in the United Kingdom is now a liability to the British, not an asset.[21]

While Northern Ireland's government may be more secularized, its two communities are not. Rather, the violence since 1968 has produced over 700 fatalities and thousands of wounded, in a population of just 1,527,593. Centuries-old hostilities have been inflamed further by the present turbulence. Protestants view the actions of the IRA as personal attacks against them and often blame Catholic citizens for supporting the IRA. The rather one-sided imposition of security measures against the Catholic community, especially prior to 1973, exacerbated their hostility toward the British and Northern Irish systems. One of the striking features of social life observed by the writer in 1973 was the even greater degree today that churches provide for the entertainment of young people. In sum, government in Northern Ireland has formally become secular; the political culture, however, has become more polarized on the basis of religious communalism.

The Limits of Secularization in the Republic

We have seen that the troubles in Northern Ireland have produced a slight degree of secularization in the Republic, perhaps more in church-state relations than in the beliefs and values of Irish citizens. Far more important to the trend toward secularization in the Republic, however, has been the radical structural changes in rural Irish society that have weakened traditional authority patterns and community networks. Also of great significance are the effects of urbanization, economic modernization, entry into the Common Market, and the impact of modern ideas by means of the electronic media and returning citizen-emigrants.

But, structural changes do not necessarily produce immediate changes in values. Nor does the introduction of new values mean the total displacement of older ones. Cultures are extremely resilient phenomena. Though a world culture may be emerging, due to modern technological advances, there remain pronounced differences between national political cultures. One need only view the differences of the West Germans, Americans, the British, and Japanese—all from similar political and economic systems—to perceive the lasting quality of national cultures. Structures change, but styles tend to endure.

Studies by Humphreys and others indicate the continuing comparative importance of Irish personalism, even in urban settings.[22] Indeed, this feature of Irish culture appears to have survived transplantation to the United States, as the earlier cited study of Irish-American policemen indicated.[23] The political and administrative style of the Irish has, also, changed only slowly. Despite the rapidly changing role of the Church, deference to clergy is perhaps greater than in any other society in the Western world. This fact was dramatically demonstrated to the writer in 1970 when, still in his twenties, he happened to wear a buttoned-up black raincoat on the frequently rainy Irish days. Old men—as well as those of his own age—would hold doors, stand aside in shops even if they had arrived first, and otherwise defer to a young man they incorrectly assumed to be a priest. Though this experience was somewhat embarrassing, and the coat was eventually traded in for a more suitable model, it occasionally and unintentionally proved advantageous when hailing a taxi, or otherwise seeking assistance. It also clearly demonstrated the continuing deference to religious authority, even in the secularized city of Dublin. The Church, then, is by no means dead in Ireland. Despite ecumenism, despite the growing role of government, and despite the changing values of the young, Ireland remains a significantly sacred, and only partially secularized, society.

The limited secularization of Irish society, however, should not necessarily be viewed as a liability. Traditional values continue to support the system, and can even be a means of legitimizing change. For example, deferential orientations toward the Church could eventually help legitimate reforms designed to assist limited long-range integration between the Republic and Northern Ireland, if Church leaders advocate, or at least accept, such changes. Above all, sacred values may help reduce the sense of detachment, alienation, and insecurity of life in modern societies. Substantial separation of church and state may be necessary for political development, but transvaluation from a sacred to a secular political culture is probably less important, and may, in extreme form, be a liability. In short, although secularization has taken place in Ireland, the society remains traditional in many important respects.

It is not inevitable, however, that secularization will match the needs of a rapidly changing Ireland. It could be too fast, too slow, or congruent with systemic needs. Many of these changes and circumstances are the result of social forces rather than conscious human direction. Yet, it remains within the power of the Irish elite to make positive efforts to support necessary change. Politics can be partially determined by leadership. despite the enormity of environmental forces. Given the situation in the North, for example, it may take strong and courageous leadership to move more rapidly than the political culture seems to allow. In fact, as noted earlier, political actions and structures can help, ultimately, to determine values.

Yet, there is a danger that political leaders will underrate the significance of residual traditional values. Today there exists a strong move toward democratization in virtually all democratic nations; it includes, among other things, the notion that true democracy is possible only where power is decentralized to local communities. More extreme demands for democratization advocate decentralizing power within nearly all organizations such as factories and places of employment. On the other hand, scholars such as T. J. Barrington and Desmond Roche make sophisticated and responsible arguments for decentralization within the context of overall programs for administrative reform.[24]

There seems little doubt that local communal decision making, with widespread participation, might constitute an improvement in the degree of democratic control on certain issues. Conceivably, some categories of important political decisions in modern societies could be decentralized—for example, zoning requirements on housing and business construction.[25] And there is little doubt that in some, though certainly not all, economic enterprises greater employee participation could not only enhance employee rights, but also could increase production. Yet several considerations need to be kept in mind.

First, many crucial decisions affecting society—foreign policy, economic policy, taxation, etc.—are necessarily central in nature. It is doubtful whether, in day-to-day matters, the public has either the interest or the capacity to make decisions. Naturally, for monumentally important issues, such as entry into the Common Market, a strong case can be made for mass participation. The referendum on Irish entry into the Common Market is an obvious example. It has previously been suggested, in fact, that the Irish electorate may be somewhat more interested and better informed than voters in most democratic nations.

The fact that decisions are made centrally does not necessarily mean that leaders are totally irresponsible. Indeed Dye and Zeigler have shown the irony of the fact that, even in the federalistic and less authoritarian American context, leaders are more democratic in their values than average citizens. Hence, lack of mass participation helps enable the system to operate more democratically. They acknowledge, of course, a number of political restraints on U. S. leaders as well as other considerations.[26] In Ireland, however, both the mass and elite political cultures are more authoritarian than their counterparts in the United States. Indeed, it is more ironic that the authoritarianism and personalism of Irish democracy have been instrumental factors in the administrative and democratic political development of Ireland. The much deeper irony of Irish democracy is that such pervasive authoritarian as well as personalistic values have constituted a fundamental support for democratic procedures and institutions.

When citizens are little interested in day-to-day administrative decisions because of their personal preoccupations and lack of information, there seems little reason to assume that they will eagerly become involved in local policy issues. Indeed, compared to the big issues of international and national politics, local issues are often rather dull. In light of the authoritarian nature of the Irish political culture, which remains rather pronounced even today, it is likely that only a few members of the local elites would dominate policy decisions. Thus, democratization of local politics could produce undemocratic rather than democratic results.

Moreover, with respect to the public service, democratization can be fundamentally undemocratic. In an age in which civil servants are acquiring an increasing role in policy making, as a result of specialization, complexity, and the sheer volume of decisions, it is essential that the public retain control of their actions. Surely this control involves supervision by elected leaders to a significant degree. Excessive participation in administrative decisions by interested parties often only leads to greater control by vested interests. Thus, top-level control of civil servants becomes crucial.[27]

Radical changes in the direction of democratization in Ireland, then, appear neither possible nor desirable. Rather, such reforms should probably be selective and limited in scope. We are not, of course, speaking of administrative decentralization, but of large-scale decentralization aimed at public participation. In fact, authoritarian norms could be used to legitimate decisions made by political leaders that would lead to further democratization of national policy and, perhaps improve relations with the North. This would naturally require courageous and democratic-minded leaders. Authoritarian and personalistic sentiments can provide leaders a freer hand, and this freedom can be used to make decisions that might not otherwise be acceptable to the Irish public. In turn, these decisions might slowly contribute to the gradual evolution of a more democratic political culture.

The relation between culture and politics is one of reciprocity. Politics are heavily constrained by cultural settings, but political leaders can change not only transient attitudes but, in time, help mold more deeply-held beliefs and values. The requirement and goal of political systems need not be the maintenance of absolute congruence between culture and politics.[28] Political leadership is, largely, the art of using existing political culture wisely, and attempting to alter it only when desirable or necessary. Gradual and selective democratization of the Irish political culture might be one example. However, sound leadership might also involve helping prevent the erosion of supportive traditional values.

7 Conclusion

The analysis of the Irish experience strongly suggests that traditional norms can contribute significantly to the early stages of political development in new nations. These findings therefore support the conclusions of several major studies in the political development literature. As the chapter on authoritarianism has demonstrated, authoritarian values can provide an important means of reducing the strain on newly independent governments by decreasing demands on the political system. They predispose the public to accept the decisions and policies of legitimate authority, which in Ireland meant accepting the decisions of native political leaders. Authoritarian norms also help in the formation of viable organizations by creating willingness to accept orders and by encouraging employee acceptance of organizational rules and goals, objectives tied closely to the achievement of political development.

But the experience of Ireland suggests that authoritarian beliefs and values are more supportive of democratic political development than is sometimes supposed. In Ireland authoritarian values supported not just political development but democratic political development as well. Thus, authoritarian norms can support more than early undemocratic stages of development in which authoritarian government provides a framework for the later establishment of a democratic polity. They also can support democratic governments in the initial stages of development, for in Ireland the government was essentially democratic from the start.

The conservatism of authoritarian values reinforced commitment to democratic procedures and processes, because conservatism reinforces existing conditions, whatever they may be. Moreover, especially after the civil war, the increased willingness of the public to follow laws and regulations reduced the need of political leaders to employ harsh enforcement techniques, and thereby facilitated the preservation of civil liberties. Students of political development, then, may be too pessimistic about the deleterious influence of authoritarian norms.

Nevertheless, one ought to remember that many social and political phenomena can have both positive and negative consequences. Obviously, excessively authoritarian public and elite values may threaten the existence of democratic politics. Indeed, it was shown that, particularly during the 1920s and 1930s, statements and actions of leaders sometimes infringed upon certain civil rights and liberties. It is clear, also, that authoritarianism can lead to the stifling of initiative within organizations, and to rigidity in the treatment of clientele. This, of course, impedes the capacity of the government to generate popular support.

In Ireland, however, a pronounced personalistic style has helped overcome negative consequences. To an unusual extent the personal style involves consulting a relative, friend, or politician who can get the job accomplished. It provides a significant link between citizen and government. Personalism also contributes to a flexible organizational style and helps in the establishment and maintenance of efficient informal organizations. It is suggested, in short, that the pronounced personalism in the Irish Republic affords a significant means of creating supportive interpersonal relations, and of overcoming the negative features of authoritarianism. Ironically, authoritarianism and personalism, together with the social institutions that support them, have been among the most important forces supporting Irish democratic development— despite the fact that these phenomena are seemingly quite undemocratic.

This study indicates that personalism need not lead to the extreme corruption or the gross unfairness found in a number of developing nations, such as many of those in Latin America. In Ireland, particularistic and diffuse social norms did not lead to self-serving administrative and political cliques, but, instead, led to a personalistic style which supported the system. Public servants did not divert significant government funds to their own use, nor did government goals become completely circumvented for the sake of personal empire-building. Rather, personalistic values and social structures were quite adaptable to modern political processes, including those of a democratic variety.

To be sure, Ireland differs significantly from many of the nations that gained independence after World War II. The Republic of Ireland possessed, from the first days of the new state, a homogeneous culture with respect to religion, and, even, language—at least to the extent that language was not a source of chronic friction for the leaders of the new state. Because there was little cultural fragmentation, and because there was a long struggle against the English, the Irish had little trouble establishing a strong popular sense of national identity. In addition, social mobilization in Ireland tended to be slow and sequential. Also, some of the most authoritarian social institutions, such as Catholicism, were linked to the struggle for democratic national sovereignty. Ireland additionally benefited from the viable and effective administrative structure developed under English auspices. Furthermore, trained Irishmen filled top administrative posts prior to independence, and public support for democratic structures carried over from the period preceding independence.

Nevertheless, Ireland at independence had many of the typical characteristics of developing nations. Its economy was underdeveloped; its leaders were inexperienced; and its stability was threatened by civil war. Above all, Ireland possessed a traditional political culture that emphasized religious, authoritarian, and personalistic values. As such, its experience may be of considerable interest to students of administrative development in Third-World areas.

One of the most interesting hypotheses generated by the present study, however, is that personalistic norms may be more appropriate and beneficial for modern nations than is usually assumed. At least, since the late 1950s, Ireland can be classified as a complex and comparatively modern nation. Yet it has remained a nation with a personalistic political and administrative style. It is apparent, moreover, that this personalism remains an important integrating and legitimizing force.

Because modern nations are plagued by increasing cultural fragmentation, mechanisms that facilitate integration are of great importance. Much of the hostility of young people, and others, toward the values of modern societies is a consequence of the depersonalizing and dehumanizing features of complex structures and universalistic norms. For, universalism requires that people be treated alike and implies that they are of value, primarily, in functional rather than in human terms. In other words, they are viewed objectively, not subjectively. Yet, surely, generalized standards ought not be rejected. The discontent generated by modern institutions is not the result of universal standards, but largely the consequence of impersonal behavior by employees of modern organizations. In other words, the problem is largely a matter of style. Administrative changes designed to generate more humane treatment of clientele, however, can also lead to more humane policies. Furthermore, universalism and equality before the law need not be sacrificed, for these characteristics are also essential for legitimacy and humaneness. One of the principal features of the Irish system is that universalistic criteria are employed in a personal fashion.

It needs to be made clear, however, that the particular kind of personalism found in Ireland cannot be adopted entirely by all modern nations. For one thing, Irish personalism is rooted in national cultural traditions. Ireland is, also, a small society with less crucial problems of geographic mobility than exist in some modern systems; family and friendship ties remain effective over long periods of time. On the other hand, not all personalistic transactions in Ireland take place among family members and old friends. Nor are all political and administrative contacts within government based on family or long-standing friendship ties. It is, rather, the style of Irish political and administrative life that is personalistic. New political or administrative recruits, for example, operate personally with newly acquired contacts—far more so than in other modern nations.

A number of organizational mechanisms or officials, other than elected representatives, might be employed to increase the personal element in dealings between the public and government agencies in modern societies. Ombudsmen already exist in some nations, but ombudsmen are after-the-fact intermediaries. It is entirely possible, however, that modern administrative systems could establish many additional procedures and structures for creating more personal relations between citizens and government and, indeed, between citizens and any organization, without sacrificing the benefit of universal criteria in the application of laws and rules. The payoff for such structurally-induced changes would be enormous. For depersonalization is a major source of the discontent and instability of contemporary societies.

Indeed, greater personalism may be more significant to the future of modern democracies than greater participation and democratization. There is no question but that some democratization would be healthy, and there is certainly substantial room for greater fairness and equality of opportunity; yet the ultimate problem for modern democracies is legitimacy, not excessive authority. Radical democratization could produce chaos and weaken governmental legitimacy through such means as creation of excessive questioning of the system and its leaders, as well as an overload of the government with demands and public pressures. The pace and rate of democratization are perhaps as crucial as its scope. In fact, democratization, while potentially a healthy phenomenon is, paradoxically, one of the greatest dangers facing modern democratic nations. For the values of democratization require significant structural and attitudinal change if there is to be greater participation and decentralization of political power. Even if mass and elite values were to change, a crucial factor would be whether or not new structures could retain the capacity and authority to coordinate and determine public policy. If they could not, the only possible alternative to chaos might be non-democratic political institutions. Even reformed democratic governments would require substantial public compliance and a generalized willingness to obey most laws. In Ireland, however, traditional values are likely to make future democratization a slow, evolutionary process. Thus, authoritarianism and personalism may very well help sustain future democratic political development in that nation.

Notes

Chapter 1
Introduction

1. For a more extended discussion of developments in the comparative field since World War II see Dankwart A. Rustow, "New Horizons for Comparative Politics," *World Politics,* vol. 9 (July 1957), 530-49. See also Gabriel A. Almond and G. Bingham Powell, *Comparative Politics: A Developmental Approach* (Boston: Little, Brown, 1966), Chapter 1.

2. A summation of the literature and an interpretation of it may be found in Samuel Huntington, "The Change to Change: Modernization, Development, and Politics," *Comparative Politics,* vol. 3 (April, 1971).

3. Alfred Diamant, "The Nature of. Political Development," in *Political Development and Social Change,* ed., Jason L. Finkle and Richard W. Gable (New York: John Wiley & Sons, Inc., 1966), p. 92. See also Leonard Binder, et. al., eds., *Crises and Sequences in Political Development* (Princeton: Princeton University Press, 1971).

4. Lucian W. Pye and Sidney Verba, eds., *Political Culture and Political Development* (Princeton, N.J.: Princeton University Press, 1965), pp. 7,8,513. Throughout the present study the term "political culture" will be used as Pye and Verba have defined it.

5. *Politics, Personality, and Nation Building: Burma's Search for Identity* (New Haven: Yale University Press, 1962), p. 52.

6. Ibid., pp. 177-86.

7. Samuel Huntington, *Political Order in Changing Societies* (New Haven: Yale University Press, 1968), p. 12.

8. Clifford Geertz, "The Integrative Revolution: Primordial Sentiments and Civic Politics in the New States," in *Old Societies and New States: The Quest for Modernity in Asia and Africa,* ed., Clifford Geertz (New York: The Free Press of Glencoe, 1963), pp. 109-19 passim.

9. *Ethnic Conflict and Political Development* (Boston: Little, Brown, 1973), p. 17 passim.

10. These terms will be defined at the beginnings of chapters 4 and 5 respectively.

11. For example, see Robert Ward, "Political Modernization and Political Culture in Japan," *World Politics,* vol. 15 (July, 1963), pp. 569-96.

Chapter 2
The Irish Social and Political Systems

1. Ireland, Central Statistics Office, *Census of Population, 1971,* vol. 1 (Dublin: Stationary Office, 1972), pp. xiv, xv, xvii. The Dublin figure is for the Dublin County Borough and does not include the Dun Laoghaire Borough.

2. Ireland, *Statistical Abstract: 1968,* p. 53. Religious data for the 1971 census were not available at this writing, but no dramatic change is anticipated.

3. *Irish Times,* March 3, 1971 report of Market Research Bureau survey.

4. For a more detailed discussion of economic planning in Ireland see Garret FitzGerald, *Planning in Ireland* (Dublin: Institute of Public Administration, 1968). See also Basil Chubb and Patrick Lynch, eds., *Economic Development and Planning* (Dublin: Institute of Public Administration, 1969).

5. United Nations, Department of Economic and Social Affairs, Statistical Office, *Statistical Yearbook: 1971* (/F. 72. 17. 1), 1972, p. 602. Greece and Malta have also fallen behind Ireland. See the U.N. *Statistical Yearbook: 1968* (E/F. 69.17. 1), 1969, p. 593.

6. Ireland, *Statistical Abstract: 1969,* pp. 47, 151.

7. Ibid., p. 149.

8. For further discussion of censorship see Michael Adams, *Censorship: The Irish Experience* (Dublin: Scepter Books, 1968).

9. Ireland, *Constitution,* art. 28.

10. Brian Farrell, *Chairman or Chief? The Role of the Taoiseach in Irish Government* (Dublin: Gill and Macmillan, 1971), p. 83.

11. James D. O'Donnell, *How Ireland is Governed* (Dublin: Institute of Public Administration, 1967), pp. 28-29.

12. M. O. Muimhneachain. *The Functions of the Department of the Taoiseach* (Dublin: Institute of Public Administration, 1960).

13. Chubb, *The Government and Politics of Ireland,* pp. 189-192. See also Farrell, *Chairman or Chief?*

14. J. L. McCracken, *Representative Government in Ireland: A Study of Dáil Eireann,* 1919-48 (London:Oxford University Press, 1958), pp. 176-77; Chubb, *The Government and Politics of Ireland,* p. 180; and Alan J. Ward, *Cabinet Government and Political Power in the Irish Republic* (Paper prepared for delivery at the 1973 Annual Conference of the American Committee for Irish Studies, Ann Arbor, Michigan, May 3-5, 1973).

15. Technically, the term "Oireachtas" includes the President as well as the Dáil and the Senate, but in common usage the term refers merely to the two houses; it is the latter usage that is employed in the present study.

16. McCracken, *Representative Government,* pp. 129-30, 168-69 and Chubb, *The Government and Politics of Ireland,* p. 198.

17. For a more extended discussion of parliamentary procedures in Ireland see McCracken, *Representative Government,* Chapter 9.

18. T. Troy, "Some Aspects of Parliamentary Questions," *Administration,* vol. 7 (Autumn, 1959), 251-59.

19. John Whyte, *Dáil Deputies: Their Work, Its Difficulties, Possible Remedies* (Dublin: Tuairim Society, Pamphlet no. 15, 1966). Assistance has increased since the publication of Whyte's study.

20. Ireland, *Constitution,* arts. 20-23. See also John McG. Smyth, *The Theory and Practice of the Irish Senate* (Dublin: Institute of Public Administration, 1972).

21. Chubb, *The Government and Politics of Ireland,* p. 206.

22. See Thomas Garvin, *The Irish Senate* (Dublin: Institute of Public Administration, 1969).

23. Ireland, *Constitution,* arts. 31-32.

24. Ibid, arts. 12-15, 26.

25. J.F.S. Ross, *The Irish Election System: What It Is and How It Works* (London: Pall Mall Press, 1959), p. 64.

26. Ibid., chapters v, vi, ix.

27. Ireland, *Constitution,* art. 18.

28. Garvin, *The Irish Senate,* pp. 88-89. See also, Chubb, *The Government and Politics of Ireland,* pp. 114-205.

29. Basil Chubb, "The Independent Member in Ireland," *Political Studies,* vol. 5 (June, 1957), 131-39, and Basil Chubb, "Going About Persecuting Civil Servants: The Role of the Irish Parliamentary Representative," *Political Studies,* vol. 11 (October, 1963), 272-86.

30. The discussion of parties benefits particularly from Maurice Manning, *Irish Political Parties: An Introduction* (Dublin: Gill and Macmillan, 1972).

31. In interviews with the writer, both Labour and Fine Gael deputies complained of other parties stealing their ideas, such as greater public support for secondary and higher education, and presenting them as their own.

32. Maurice Duverger, *Political Parties: Their Organization and Activities in the Modern State,* trans. by Barbara and Robert North (New York: Wiley and Sons, 1954).

33. For a discussion of the importance of the Gaelic League for Irish nationalism see Donall O'Corcora, *What's This About the Gaelic League?* (Dublin: Gaelic League, 1942).

34. *State-Sponsored Bodies* (2nd ed. rev. Dublin: Institute of Public Administration, 1963), p. 3.

35. Ibid. p. 71.

36. Survey conducted during 1972 under the auspices of The Institute of Public Administration.

37. This point will be more fully discussed in a later chapter.

38. For a discussion of the relations between interest groups and political development see Almond and Powell, *Comparative Politics: A Developmental Approach.*

39. For a theoretical discussion of direct relevance to this point see William S. Livingston, "A Note on the Nature of Federalism," *Political Science Quarterly,* vol. 67 (March, 1952), 81-95.

40. Enid Lakeman, "A Sense of Proportion: The Irish General Election, 1965," *Contemporary Review,* vol. 206 (May, 1965), 229-33. For survey data on voter interest in politics and other relevant matters see "Gallup Poll," *Nusight* (October 1969, December 1969, and April 1970).

41. D. E. Leon, *Advisory Bodies in Irish Government* (Dublin: Institute of Public Administration, 1963).

42. For a theoretical discussion of interest-group influence see Graham Wootton, *Interest Groups,* (Englewood Cliffs, N.J.: Prentice-Hall, 1970).

43. The major study on church-state relations is by John Whyte, *Church and State in Modern Ireland, 1923-1970,* (Dublin: Gill and Macmillan, 1971).

44. The Vatican Councils and recent papal encyclicals have had a significant liberalizing influence on the Irish hierarchy. The writer is currently completing an article on the Church's modernizing role.

45. Ireland, *Statistical Abstract: 1968,* p. 45.

46. Various members of the Irish bureaucracy, including one top official of a highly-relevant government department, also maintained that the military had little policy-making voice. Of course, since the violence in Northern Ireland flared up, the inputs of the military into policy in foreign affairs have undoubtedly increased, and the military has engaged in various small-scale operations. But there is little doubt that civilian politicians remain in control. Donald E. Leon is now completing detailed research on the role of the military in Irish politics, and his published findings will undoubtedly add greatly to the understanding of the military's role

47. "The Turnover Tax," *New Statesman,* November 8, 1963, pp. 640-41. See also "Taxing the Irish Way," *Economist,* April 2, 1966, pp. 66-67. Of course, entry into the Common Market will alter the tax structure, but that tax structure will not become radically progressive in nature.

48. For a discussion of Irish welfare policy see P. R. Kaim-Caudle, *Social Policy in the Irish Republic* (London: Routledge and Kegan Paul, 1967).

Chapter 3
Irish Political Development: Institutionalization
and Social Mobilization

1. The definition with an important analysis will be found in Karl W. Deutsch, "Social Mobilization and Political Development," *American Political*

Science Review, vol. 55 (September, 1961), pp. 463-515.

2. For a discussion of these and other problems see Ibid. and Huntington *Political Order,* Passim.

3. For an interesting typology and analysis of different patterns of development see C. E. Black, *The Dynamics of Modernization: A Study in Comparative History* (New York: Harper and Row, 1966). See also Eric Nordlinger, "Political Development: Time sequences and Rates of Change," *World Politics,* vol. 20 (April, 1968), 494-520.

4. For a more detailed discussion of early Irish history see Edmund Curtis, *A History of Ireland* (6th ed. London: Methuen & Co., 1950) and T. W. Moody and F. X. Martin, eds., *The Course of Irish History* (New York: Weybright and Talley, 1966).

5. Curtis, *A History of Ireland,* pp. 358-63.

6. For a more complete analysis of the repeal movement see Kevin B. Nowlan, *The Politics of Repeal: A Study in the Relations Between Great Britain and Ireland, 1841-50* (London: Routledge & Kegan Paul, 1965. Toronto: University of Toronto Press, 1965).

7. For an excellent discussion of the importance of British political institutions for Irish political development see Brian Farrell's article "The New State and Irish Political Culture," *Administration,* 16 (Autumn, 1968), 238-46. See also, his book, *The Founding of Dáil Eireann* (Dublin: Gill and Macmillan, 1971).

8. The nineteenth century was also a period of great reform for public administration in England. For example, the British Civil Service Commission was established in 1855, and by 1870 most white-collar entrants into the public service were recruited by examination. For a discussion see Ivor Jennings, *The Queen's Government* (rev. Baltimore: Penquin Books, 1965), pp. 104-108.

9. R. B. McDowell, *The Irish Administration, 1801-1914* (London: Routledge & Kegan Paul, 1964. Toronto: University of Toronto Press, 1964), chapter 1 Passim.

10. For an analysis of the period from 1840 to independence see Nicholas Mansergh, *The Irish Question: 1840-1921* (rev. Toronto: University of Toronto Press, 1965). For a discussion of the decline of the Irish party see F. S. L. Lyons, *The Irish Parliamentary Party, 1890-1910* (London: Faber and Faber, Ltd., 1951). For an important treatment of the entire period see F. S. L. Lyons, *Ireland Since the Famine* (New York: Charles Scribner's Sons, 1971).

11. Great Britain, *Census of Ireland, 1911: General Report* (London: His Majesty's Stationery Office, 1913), pp. 1,291.

12. Mary Hayden and George A. Moonan, *A Short History of the Irish People, pt. 3: From 1603 to Modern Times* (rev. Dublin: Educational Company of Ireland, 1960), pp. 264-65.

13. For a breakdown on the size of Irish farms see Great Britain, *Census of Ireland, 1911*, pp. lxi-lxii, 439.

14. Ibid.

15. Ibid., p. 42.

16. Donald Akenson, *The Irish Education Experiment: The National System of Education in the Nineteenth Century* (London: Routledge & Kegan Paul, 1970. Toronto: University of Toronto Press, 1970), pp. 238-39 376, 389 Passim.

17. See Robert Lynd, *Home Life in Ireland* (London: Mills & Boon, 1909), pp. 91-94, 106-107.

18. L. Paul-Dubois, *Contemporary Ireland* (Dublin: Maunsel and Company, 1908), p. 91.

19. Desmond Farley, *Social Insurance and Social Assistance in Ireland* (Dublin: Institute of Public Administration), pp. vii-xii, 1-7.

20. J. Meghen, "Social History" in *The Limerick Rural Survey*, Jeremiah Newman, ed. (Tipperary: Muintirnatir Rural Publications, 1964), p. 156.

21. Ibid., pp. 149, 155.

22. See Patrick Lynch, "The Social Revolution that Never Was," in *The Irish Struggle: 1916-1926*, Desmond Williams, ed. (London: Routledge and Kegan Paul, 1966), pp. 41-54. See also Farrell, "The New State."

23. Donal McCartney, "Gaelic Ideological Origens of 1916," in *1916: The Easter Rising*, O. Dudley Edwards and Fergus Pyle, eds. (London: MacGibbon & Kee, 1968), pp. 41-49.

24. See, for example, "The Murder Machine " by the revolutionary hero Padraic H. Pearse, reprinted in the book of his works entitled *Political Writings and Speeches* (Dublin: The Talbot Press, 1952).

25. See P. S. Dineen, *Native History in Irish Schools* (Dublin: M. H. Gill & Son, 1905).

26. "Gaelic Ideological Origens," p. 45.

27. *Ireland in the New Century* (London: John Murray, 1905), p. 150. See also Arland Ussher, *The Face and Mind of Ireland* (London: Victor Collancz, 1949), pp. 26-27 and Brian Inglis, *The Story of Ireland* (London: Faber and Faber, 1956), p. 95.

28. McCartney, "Gaelic Ideology," p. 46.

29. Leo Kohn, *The Constitution of the Irish Free State* (London: George Allen & Unwin, 1932), p. 30.

30. Ussher, *The Face and Mind of Ireland*, p. 26.

31. Quoted in George Arthur, *General Sir John Maxwell* (London: Murray, 1932), p. 268.

32. Timothy M. Healy, *Letters and Leaders of My Day* (London: Butterworth, 1928), vol. 2, 573, and Lyons, *The Irish Parliamentary Party*, pp. 263-64.

33. R. Dudley Edwards, "Church and State in Modern Ireland," in *Ireland in the War Years and After,* Kevin B. Nolan and T. Desmond Williams, eds., (Dublin: Gill and Macmillan, 1969), p. 109.

34. For example, the Dáil Eireann Government instituted an operational court system. See Dáil Eireann, *Official Report,* August 16, 1921–August 26, 1921, p. 22.

35. Today the full name of the British nation is still the United Kingdom of Great Britain and Northern Ireland. To this day the Irish question remains unsettled.

36. Nicholas Mansergh, *Ireland in the Age of Reform and Revolution: A Commentary on Anglo-Irish Relations and on Political Forces in Ireland,* 1840-1921 (London: George Allen & Unwin, 1940), pp. 196-204.

37. For sophisticated discussions of these and other aspects of the independence movement see Farrell, "The New State," and Lynch, "The Social Revolution." The writer also benefited from an unpublished paper by J. G. A. Pocock of the Department of History, Washington University, entitled "The Case of Ireland Truly Stated: Revolutionary Politics in the Context of Increasing Stabilization," (1966).

38. Saorstat Eireann, *Census of Population, 1926,* vol. 10: General Report (Dublin: Stationery Office, 1934), p. 48.

39. Saorstat Eireann, *Census, 1926,* Vol. 10, 71. On Protestantism, consult Michael Hurley, S. J., ed. *Irish Anglicanism; 1869-1969* (Dublin: Allen Figgis, 1970).

40. Denis Gwynn, *The Irish Free State, 1922-1927* (London: Macmillan, 1928), p. 273. Gwynn's book is the best single analysis available for readers concerned with developmental problems faced by the new Free State Government, and it was of great benefit in writing the present section of the third chapter.

41. For a discussion of the treaty and its implications see Kohn, *The Constitution of the Irish Free State,* chapter 4. On the civil war, see Calton Younger, *A State of Disunion* (London: Frederick Muller, 1972) and Eoin Neeson, *The Civil War in Ireland* (Cork: Mercier Press, 1966). In general, the more nationalistic secions tended to be the West and the poorer sections of Irish society. See E. Rumpf, *Nationalismus und Sozialismus in Irland.* Meisenheim am Glan, 1959.

42. Saorstat Eireann, *Parliamentary Debates,* vol. 3, 2003.

43. See, for example, Michael Cardinal Logue, "The Voice of the Church on Internal Strife," in *The Voice of Ireland: A Survey of the Race and Nation From All Angles,* William G. Fitz-Gerald, ed. (Manchester: John Heywood, 1924), pp. 275-76.

44. Gwynn, *The Irish Free State,* chapter 12. Also, Donald Leon's new study should shed further light on the role of the military.

45. *The Legitimacy of Opposition: The Change of Government in Ireland in 1932.* Paper prepared for delivery at the 1966 Annual Meeting of the American

Political Science Association, New York City, September 6-10, 1966.

46. For one of the most important studies of this period see Maurice Manning, *The Blueshirts* (Toronto: University of Toronto Press, 1971).

47. Chubb, *The Government: An Introduction;* and D. H. Akenson and J. F. Fallin, "The Irish Civil War and the Drafting of the Free State Constitution," *Eire-Ireland,* vol. 5 (Summer, 1970), 42-93, and (Winter, 1970), 28-70.

48. For analyses of the Constitution of the Irish Free State as well as the operation of the structures of the Free State government in practice see Nicholas Mansergh, *The Irish Free State: Its Government and Politics* (London: George Allen and Unwin, 1934), and Kohn, *The Constitution of the Irish Free State.*

49. Saorstat Eireann, *Commission of Enquiry into Civil Service, 1932-35* (Dublin: Stationery Office, 1935), p. 3.

50. Ibid., pp. 3, 138.

51. See Thomas P. Linehan, "The Growth of the Civil Service," *Administration,* vol. 2 (Summer, 1954), 61.

52. Farrell, "The New State," and *The Founding of Dáil Eireann.*

53. *The Irish Parliamentary Party,* pp. 67-68.

54. *The Constitution of the Irish Free State,* p. 112.

55. Saorstat Eireann, *Constitution,* art. 7.

56. Ibid., arts, v, ix, xv.

57. Quoted in Donal O'Sullivan, *The Irish Free State and Its Senate: A Study in Contemporary Politics* (London: Faber and Faber, 1940), p. 61.

58. Saorstat Eireann, *Parliamentary Debates,* vol. 22, 1615.

59. Ibid.

60. Saorstat Eireann, *Parliamentary Debates,* vol. 28, 1399.

61. On party development see Warner Moss, *Political Parties in the Irish Free State* (New York: Columbia University Press, 1933).

62. Saorstat Eireann, *Reports of the Fiscal Inquiry Committee* (Dublin: Stationery Office, 1923), and *Parliamentary Debates,* vol. 3, 2022-2025.

63. Gwynn, *The Irish Free State,* Pt. 3.

64. Kohn, *The Constitution of the Irish Free State,* p. 112.

65. (Dublin: Stationery Office, December, 1967), p. 4.

66. Ireland, *Census of Population of Ireland, 1966,* 1, xiii.

67. Although available comparative data on the percentage of change in the distribution of population in rural and urban areas is somewhat imprecise, the pattern of relatively slow urbanization is clear; see Ibid., pp. xii-xiii and table iv, p. xiii for comparative figures. Data on occupations also indicates fairly slow patterns of change from agricultural to industrial and related occupations. See Ireland, *Statistical Abstract of Ireland, 1968* (Dublin: Stationery Office, 1968), pp. 45-49, and Eire, *Census of Population, 1936*

(Dublin: Stationery Office, 1940), 7, 2-15.

68. *Politics, Personality, and Nation Building* pp. 38-42, 51-52. Passim.

Chapter 4
Irish Authoritarianism

1. *The Moral Basis of a Backward Society* (Glencoe, Ill.: The Free Press, 1958) Passim. See Laurence Wylie, *Village in the Vaucluse* (Cambridge: Harvard University Press, 1957), for another example of hostile cultural values in Europe. For an oriental illustration consult Pye, *Politics, Personality and Nation Building.*

2. For example, Ward, "Political Modernization."

3. Pye, *Politics, Personality, and Nation Building,* p. 51.

4. Fred W. Riggs's classic study *Thailand: The Modernization of a Bureaucratic Polity* (Chicago: University of Chicago Press, 1964) provides an excellent example of bureaucratic dominance.

5. For a brief discussion of some of the early techniques see D. A. Binchy, "Secular Institutions," in *Early Irish Society,* Myles Dillon, ed. (Dublin: Colm O'Lochlainn for the Cultural Relations Committee of Ireland, 1954), pp. 52-65.

6. *Ireland in the New Century* (London: John Murray, 1905), p. 212. See also L. Paul-Dubois, *Contemporary Ireland* (Dublin: Maunsel and Company, 1908), p. 166.

7. James Q. Wilson, "Generational and Ethnic Differences Among Career Police Officers," *American Journal of Sociology* vol. 59 (March, 1964), 522-528.

8. Ian Hart, "Public Opinion on Civil Servants and the Role and Power of the Individual in the Community," *Administration,* vol. 18 (Winter, 1970), pp. 377-78. Compared with British and United States citizens, however, Dubliners were somewhat less trusting of police. This can be explained by Ireland's history of foreign domination and repression. Hart's study shows Dubliners to be more trusting of police than are the citizens of Italy, West Germany, and Mexico.

9. Donald S. Connery, *The Irish* (New York: Simon and Schuster, 1968).

10. A discussion of the findings will be found in Richard E. Dawson and Kenneth Prewitt, *Political Socialization* (Boston: Little, Brown, 1969).

11. Conrad M. Arensberg and Solon T. Kimball, *Family and Community in Ireland* (Cambridge, Mass.: Harvard University Press, 1940), pp. 79-97 Passim.

12. Damian Hannan, "Kinship, Neighborhood and Social Change in Irish Rural Communities," *Economic and Social Review,* vol. 3 (January, 1972), 163-88.

13. Alexander J. Humphreys, *New Dubliners* (London: Routledge and Kegan Paul, 1966), p. 250.

14. McNabb, "Social Structure," p. 228. See also Caoimhin O'Danachair, "The Family in Irish Tradition," *Christus Rex,* vol. 16 (July, August, September, 1962), pp. 185-96.

15. Humphreys, *New Dubliners,* pp. 19, 145-48, 236, 239.

16. McNabb, "Social Structure," p. 225, and O'Danachair, "The Family," pp. 185-96.

17. Timothy P. Coogan, *Ireland Since the Rising* (New York: Praeger, 1966), p. 179, and Humphreys, *New Dubliners,* pp. 20, 162.

18. "Social Structure," p. 230.

19. *Home Life in Ireland* (London: Mills & Boon, 1909), pp. 41-43.

20. Ethna Viney, "Women in Rural Ireland," *Christus Rex,* vol. 22 (October, November, December, 1968), p. 334.

21. Conrad Arensberg, *The Irish Countryman: An Anthropoligical Study* (London: Macmillan, 1937), p. 139, and Arensberg and Kimball, *Family and Community,* pp. 158, 168, 191 Passim.

22. O'Danachair, "The Family," p. 190.

23. Ibid.

24. Michael Viney, *Growing Old in Ireland* (Dublin: The Irish Times, n.d.), p. 4 Passim.

25. For data see Bertram Hutchinson, *Social Status and Inter-Generational Social Mobility in Dublin* (Dublin: The Economic and Social Research Institute, October, 1969).

26. Ibid., p. 31 passim. See also Humphreys, *New Dubliners,* p. 195.

27. See Mark Bence-Jones, *The Remarkable Irish: Chronicle of a Land, a Culture, a Mystique* (New York: McKay Co., 1966), p. 64.

28. *Ireland in the New Century,* pp. 94-95.

29. Jean Blanchard, *The Church in Contemporary Ireland* (Dublin: Clomore and Reynolds, 1963), p. 69.

30. For one such ranking see Ibid. pp. 73-74. Of course, clergy are also accorded high formal status in many other democracies.

31. *Ireland Since the Rising,* p. 213.

32. Art. 44.

33. The best source on the changing role of the Church remains the earlier cited *Church and State in Modern Ireland* by John Whyte. See also John V. Kelleher, "Ireland: And Where Does She Stand?" *Foreign Affairs,* vol. 35 (April, 1957), p. 488, and Chubb, *The Government and Politics of Ireland,* pp. 100-104.

34. Desmond Wilson, "The Priest and the Community," *Christus Rex,* vol. 20 (January, February, March, 1966), p. 46.

35. *The Face and Mind of Ireland* (London: Gollancz, 1949), p. 77.

36. For a discussion of the structure of Irish education see T. J. McElligott, *Education in Ireland* (Dublin: Institute of Public Administration, 1966). See also Norman Atkinson, *Irish Education: A History of Educational*

Institutions (Dublin: Allen Figgis, 1969).

37. For a literary illustration of authoritarianism in Irish education prior to the independence movement see James Joyce, *Portrait of the Artist as a Young Man* (New York: The Viking Press, 1961).

38. "The Christian and the Civil Service," *Administration*, vol. 3, No. 2-3, 69-74.

39. *Education and Political Development* (Princeton, N.J.: Princeton University Press, 1965), pp. 19-20, 23.

40. Ireland, Department of Education, *Rules and Programme for Secondary Schools, 1969-70* (Dublin: Stationery Office, 1970), p. 110.

41. Ibid.

42. J. McKenna et al., "The Teaching of History in Irish Schools," *Administration*, vol. 15 (Winter, 1967), pp. 268-85.

43. Survey conducted in 1972 under the auspices of the Institute of Public Administration.

44. Reported in Hart, "Public Opinion on Civil Servants," p. 386.

45. The data from this survey project are maintained at The Economic and Social Research Institute, Burlington Road, Dublin, Ireland.

46. *Irish Times,* March 31, 1973, p. 11.

47. The writer is indebted to Professor M. Donald Hancock of the University of Texas for discussion on this matter. Although Harry Eckstein's "Theory of a stable Democracy" in his book *Division and Cohesion in Democracy: A Study of Norway* (Princeton: Princeton University Press, 1966) was read after the theses of the present book were generated in 1967, it proved to be quite useful heuristically in modifying and adding points to the present work. See also his recent preliminary report on research on authority patterns. "Authority Patterns and Governmental Performance: A Theoretical Framework,"*Comparative Political Studies,* vol. 2 (October, 1969), 269-325.

48. Edward J. Williams, "Latin American Catholicism and Political Integration," *Comparative Political Studies,* vol. 2 (October, 1969), p. 342.

49. Ibid., p. 329. See also Farrell, *The Founding of Dáil Eireann,* pp. xvii-xix.

50. *The Moral Basis,* p. 8.

51. See the *Report of Public Services Organization Review Group, 1966-1969* (The Devlin Report), (Dublin: Stationery office, 1969), and "More Local Government: A Programme for Development," *Administration,* vol. 19, (Summer, 1971), 140-206.

Chapter 5
Irish Personalism

1. T. A. Callanan (in collaboration with Rev. Fr. H. Bohan), "Regional Planning: The Role of the Clergy in a Society in a Dynamic State, with Particular Reference to the Mid-West Region—The View of the Planner," *Social Studies,* vol. 1 (October, 1972), 556.

2. This literature and the strengths and limitations of the patron-client concept are discussed in Robert R. Kaufman, *The Patron-Client Concept and Macro-Politics: Prospects and Problems.* Paper prepared for delivery at the 1972 Annual Meeting of the American Political Science Association, Washington, D.C., September 4-9, 1972.

3. Gabriel Almond and Sidney Verba. *The Civic Culture: Political Attitudes and Democracy in Five Nations* (Boston: Little, Brown, 1963).

4. Talcott Parsons and Edward A. Shils, *Toward a General Theory of Action* (New York: Harper and Row, 1951), pp. 81-82 Passim.

5. For an analysis of early Irish history see Curtis, *A History of Ireland.*

6. P. Pentony, *Psychological Barriers to Economic Achievement* (Dublin: Economic and Social Research Institute, February, 1965), paper no. 25.

7. *Contemporary Ireland,* pp. 158-161.

8. *Ireland in the New Century,* pp. 166-67.

9. *Family and Community in Ireland,* Passim.

10. "Man and Kin in Donnegal: A Study of Kinship Functions in a Rural Irish and an Irish-American Community," *Ethnology,* vol. 7 (July, 1968), 245-58.

11. "Kinship, Neighborhood, and Social Change."

12. For an unsympathetic view of the civil service in contemporary Ireland see Charles McCarthy, *The Distasteful Challenge* (Dublin: Institute of Public Administration, 1968).

13. *New Dubliners,* p. 234.

14. Ibid., p. 250.

15. (Dublin: Maunsel and Company, 1918).

16. *The Irish,* p. 95.

17. A. S. Cohan, *The Irish Political Elite* (Dublin: Gill and Macmillan, 1972), p. 70.

18. One of the best comparative studies on administrative style remains Michael Crozier, *The Bureaucratic Phenomenon* (Chicago: University of Chicago Press, 1964). For Irish behavior see Whyte, *Dáil Deputies.*

19. Mart Bax, "Patronage Irish Style: Irish Politicians as Brokers," *Sociologische Gids,* vol. 17 (1970), 179-91.

20. "Sons and Widows," *Economist,* March 20, 1965, p. 1259.

21. Chubb, *The Government and Politics of Ireland,* p. 159.

22. "Balliwicks, Locality, and Religion: Three Elements in an Irish Dáil Constituency Election," *Economic and Social Review,* vol. 1 (July, 1970), 45.

23. Ibid.

24. Brian Farrell, "Dail Deputies: The 1969 Generation," *Economic and Social Review,* vol. 2 (April, 1971), 320-23.

25. Chubb, *The Government and Politics of Ireland,* p. 158. See also

Basil Chubb, "The Independent Member in Ireland," *Political Studies,* vol. 5 (June, 1957), 131-39.

26. See Farrell, "Dáil Deputies," pp. 319-20.

27. "Public Opinion on Civil Servants," p. 385.

28. Ibid. Specifically, they were asked: "Suppose a regulation were being considered by the Corporation which you thought unjust or harmful. What would you do?"

29. Economic and Social Review Project. Other responses to these two questions included stirring up public opinion, organizing protest demonstrations, voting in the next election, organizing or signing a petition, and contacting administrators. For data on responses in other democracies see Almond and Verba, *The Civic Culture.*

30. *The Distasteful Challenge* and *Public Services Organization Review Group.*

Chapter 6
Secularization and The Impact of the Northern Ireland Crisis

1. For one of the most important discussions of these and other problems, see Leonard Binder et al., *Crises and Sequences in Political Development.*

2. Donald E. Smith, *Religion and Political Development* (Boston: Little, Brown, 1970), p. 2.

3. Ibid., Chapter 4.

4. *Comparative Politics: A Developmental Approach,* p. 24.

5. *Innish Killane: Change and Decline in the West of Ireland* (London: Allen Lane, The Penquin Press, 1973).

6. Ibid., p. 36.

7. *Church and State in Modern Ireland,* Passim.

8. For a discussion of overall forces for change see Connery, *The Irish,* p. 37 Passim. Consult also Coogan, *Ireland Since the Rising.*

9. An excellent account of one crucial aspect of the events leading up to partition is A. T. Q. Stewart, *The Ulster Crisis* (London: Faber and Faber, 1967).

10. Northern Ireland, *The Ulster Year Book: The Official Handbook of Northern Ireland* (Belfast: H. M. S. O., 1972), p. 10.

11. For a critical discussion see M. W. Heslinga, *The Irish Border as a Cultural Divide: A Contribution to the Study of Regionalism in the British Isles* (Assen, The Netherlands: Van Gorcum, 1971). See also J. C. Beckett, *The Making of Modern Ireland: 1603-1923* (London: Faber and Faber, 1966).

12. Ian Budge and Cornelius O'Leary, *Belfast: Approach to Crisis, A Study of Belfast Politics 1613-1970* (London: Macmillan, 1973), and Andrew Boyd, *Holy War in Belfast: A History of the Troubles in Northern Ireland*

(New York: Grove Press, 1969).

13, Arts. 2,3.

14. See the Republic's constitution, art. 41, on divorce. Other limitations are discussed in Whyte, *Church and State in Modern Ireland.*

15. These disabilities included disadvantages in voting at local elections, gross cases of gerrymandering, and discrimination in public and private employment. Among the many documentary accounts of these and other grievances, as well as the causes of the increasing militancy of the confrontations, see Great Britain, Government of Northern Ireland, *Disturbances in Northern Ireland* (The Cameron Report), Cmd. 532 (Belfast: H. M. S. O., 1969).

16. Great Britain, *Northern Ireland Constitutional Proposals,* Cmnd. 5259 (London: H. M. S. O., 1973), pp. 29-30.

17. A poll conducted by Irish Marketing Surveys in 1973 showed that only thirty-seven percent in the Republic saw unification between North and South as the best solution to the Northern Ireland problem. Of course, respondents were given a number of options that may have colored the results. Nevertheless, it seems clear that there is not overwhelming support in the Republic for unification. Reported in the *Irish Independent,* March 5, 1973, p. 9.

18. Offences Against the State Act, 1939; Offences Against the State (Amendment) Act, 1940; and Offences Against the State (Amendment) Act, 1972.

19. See Sunday Times Insight Team, *Ulster* (Baltimore: Penquin Books, 1972), chapter 11.

20. See Cynthia H. Enloe, *Ethnic Conflict and Political Development* (Boston: Little, Brown, 1973); Conor Cruise O'Brien, *States of Ireland* (London: Hutchinson & Co., 1972; and Rose, *Governing Without Consensus* (Boston: Beacon Press, 1971). For a view emphasizing economic aspects see Liam de Paor, *Divided Ulster* (2nd ed., Middlesex, England: Penguin Books, 1972).

21. An account of Britain's deepening involvement to the point of Direct Rule is Henry Kelly, *How Stormont Fell* (Dublin: Gill and MacMillan, 1972). Northern Ireland is no longer an economic asset; indeed, it is a liability, being subsidized by the U. K. treasury, including payment of damages caused by the unrest, welfare services, etc. It is of no crucial military or strategic significance, and it is the source of great international embarrassment.

22. *New Dubliners.* For rural settings see also Kane, "Man and Kin," p. 252, which notes the importance of kinship ties" . . . as an instrument of introduction to new geographic and/or economic situations."

23. Chapter 4, note 7. However, a study by Andrew W. Greeley and William C. McCready, "An Ethnic Group Which Vanished: The Strange Case of the American Irish," *Social Studies,* vol. 1 (January, 1972), 38-50, suggests

the possibility that in other behavioral areas there may be significant cultural change among the American Irish.

24. See Barrington, "Is There a Future for the District?" *Administration,* vol. 19 (Winter, 1971), 299-317; and Desmond Roche, "Local Government Reorganization," *Administration,* vol. 19 (Winter, 1971), 318-327. See also Institute of Public Administration, "More Local Government: A Programme for Development."

25. Local zoning in the United States, however, has often helped produce racial discrimination and other abuses.

26. Thomas R. Dye and L. Harmon Zeigler, *The Irony of Democracy: An Uncommon Introduction to American Politics* (Belmont, California: Wadsworth, 1970).

27. An excellent discussion of some of these issues may be found in Emmette Redford, *Democracy in the Administrative State* (London and New York: Oxford University Press,1969),pp. 173-175 passim.

28. See Eckstein, "A Theory of Stable Democracy."

Selected Bibliography

Documentary Sources

Chubb, Basil, ed. *A Source Book of Irish Government.* Dublin: Institute of Public Administration, 1964.

Flynn, William J., ed. *Free State Parliamentary Companion for 1932.* Dublin: Talbot Press, 1932.

——————, ed. *Irish Parliamentary Handbook: 1939.* Dublin: Stationery Office, 1939.

——————, ed. *The Oireachtas Companion and Saorstat Guide for 1929.* Dublin: Hely's, 1929.

Great Britain. *Census of Ireland, 1911.* London: Stationery Office, 1913.

——————. *Northern Ireland Constitutional Proposals.* London: Stationery Office, 1973, Cmnd. 5259.

——————. *Report of the Enquiry into Allegations Against the Security Forces of Physical Brutality in Northern Ireland Arising Out of Events on the 9th August, 1971* (The Compton Report). London: Stationery Office, 1971. Cmnd. 4823.

Ireland. *Census of Population, 1926.* Dublin: Stationery Office, 1926.

——————. *Census of Population, 1961.* Dublin: Stationery Office, 1963.

——————. Central Statistics Office. *Census of Population, 1971,* vol. 1. Dublin: Stationery Office, 1972.

——————. Central Statistics Office. *Statistical Abstract of Ireland, 1968.* Dublin: Stationery Office, 1968.

——————. Central Statistics Office. *Statistical Abstract, 1969.* Dublin: Stationery Office, 1971.

——————. *Commission of Inquiry into the Civil Service: 1932-1935.* Dublin: Stationery Office, 1935.

——————. *Constitution of the Irish Free State.* Dublin: Stationery Office. 1922.

——————. *Constitution* (Bunreacht na hEireann). Dublin: Stationery Office, 1938.

——————. Dáil Eireann. *Dáil Debates,* vol. 3 (12 April-2 July, 1923.)

——————. Dáil Eireann. *Official Report,* vol. 1 (16 August-26 August 1921 and 28 February-8 June, 1922).

97

Ireland. Dáil Eireann. *Parliamentary Debates,* vol. 28 (20 February—22 March 1929).

_____. Department of External Affairs. *Facts about Ireland.* Dublin: Stationery Office, 1963.

_____. Department of Finance. *Economic Development.* Dublin: Stationery Office, 1958.

_____. Department of Finance. *Report of Public Services Organization Review Group: 1966-1969.* Dublin: Stationery Office, 1969.

_____. Department of Finance. *Review of 1966 and Outlook for 1967, Incorporating Economic Statistics for 1967.* Dublin: Stationery Office, 1967.

_____. Department of Industry and Commerce. *Census of the Population, 1926.* Dublin: Stationery Office, 1928.

_____. Department of Local Government and Public Health. *Report: 1931-32.* Dublin: Stationery Office, 1933.

_____. Department of Local Government and Public Health. *Second Report: 1925-1927.* Dublin: Stationery Office, 1928.

_____. Government Information Bureau. *Irish Unity, Northern Ireland, Anglo-Irish Relations: August 1969-October 1971* (Speeches by the Taoiseach, John Lynch). Dublin: Stationery Office, 1971.

_____. *Local Government Reorganization* (White Paper). Dublin: Stationery Office, 1971.

_____. *Programme for Economic Expansion.* Dublin: Stationery Office, 1958.

_____. *Regional Studies in Ireland.* Dublin: An Foras Forbartha, 1968.

_____. *Report and Advisory Outline Plan for the Limerick Region.* Dublin: Stationery Office, 1967.

_____. *Report of the Commission on the Relief of the Sick and Destitute Poor, Including the Insane Poor.* Dublin: Stationery Office, 1927.

_____. *Report of the Committee on the Constitution* Dublin: Stationery Office, 1967.

_____. *Report of Public Services Review Group, 1966-1969* (the Devlin Report). Dublin; Stationery Office, 1969.

_____. *Reports of the Fiscal Inquiry Committee.* Dublin: Stationery Office, 1923.

_____. *Second Programme for Economic Expansion, pt. 1.* Dublin: Stationery Office, 1963.

_____. *Second Programme for Economic Expansion, pt. 2.* Dublin: Stationery Office, 1964.

_____. *Strengthening the Local Government Service.* Dublin: Stationery Office, 1971.

_____. *Third Programme: Economic and Social Development, 1969-72.* Dublin: Stationery Office, 1969.

Northern Ireland. *Disturbances in Northern Ireland* (the Cameron Report). Belfast: Stationery Office, 1969. Cmd. 532.

_____. *A Record of Constructive Change.* Belfast: Stationery Office, 1971. Cmd. 558.

United Nations. Department of Economic add Social Affairs. Statistical Office. *Demographic Yearbook: 1968* (E/F. 69.17.1), 1969.

_____. Department of Economic and Social Affairs. Statistical Office. *Statistical Yearbook: 1968* (E/F.69.17.1), 1969.

Articles and Periodicals

Akenson, D. H. and Fallin, J. F. "The Irish Civil War and the Drafting of the Free State Constitution," *Eire-Ireland,* 5 (Summer, 1970), 42-93, and (Winter, 1970), 28-70.

Almond, Gabriel A. "Political Development: Analytical and Normative Perspectives." *Comparative Political Studies,* 1 (January, 1969), 447-69.

Barrington, T. J. "Is There a Future For the District?"*Administration,* 19 (Winter, 1971), 299-317.

_____. "National Development and Local Government." *Administration,* 10 (Winter, 1962), 352-62.

_____. "The Structure of the Civil Service: Elaborate Contrivance." *Administration,* 3 (Summer-Autumn, 1955), 94-108.

Bax, Mart. "Patronage Irish Style: Irish Politicians as Brokers." *Sociologische Gids,* 17 (1970), 179-191.

Best, Ernest. "Elections in Erie." *Christian Century,* 78 (December 6, 1961), 1474-75.

Binchy, D. A. "Secular Institutions." *Early Irish Society.* Myles Dillon, ed. Dublin: Colm O'Lochlainn, 1954.

Bromage, Arthur W. "The Council-Manager Plan in Ireland." *Administration,* 9 (Winter, 1961-62), 309-317.

_____. "Irish Councilmen at Work." *Administration,* 2 (Spring, 1954), 87-96.

Callanan, T. A. "Regional Planning: The Role of the Clergy in a Dynamic State, with Particular Reference to the Mid-West Region—The View of the Planner," *Social Studies,* 1 (October, 1972).

"Censoring the Telefis." *Economist,* October 22, 1966, 363.

"Changes in Social Security Legislation in Ireland." *International Labour Review,* 89 (June, 1964), 605-606.

Chase, Eugene P. "More Education for Ireland." *Administration,* 10 (Winter, 1962), 346-51.

Chubb, Basil. "Cabinet Government in Ireland." *Political Studies,* 3 (October, 1955), 256-74.

_____. "Going About Persecuting Civil Servants: the Role of the Irish Parliamentary Representative." *Political Studies,* 11 (October, 1963), 272-86.

_____. "The Independent Member in Ireland." *Political Studies,* 5 (June, 1957), 131-39.

_____. "Public Control of Public Enterprise." *Administration,* 2 (Spring, 1954), 21-32.

Cockburn, Claud. "Confident Mood of the New Ireland." *New York Times Magazine,* January 14, 1962, pp. 28-32.

Condon, D. "Executive Thinking—A Survey." *Administration,* 2 (Spring, 1954), 75-86.

"Conference of the Irish Congress of Trade Unions." *International Labour Review,* 91 (February, 1965), 160-62.

Connolly, Michael. "Democracy." *The Irish Monthly,* 82 (February, 1953), 43-48.

Coughlan, Anthony. "Public Affairs, 1916-1966: The Social Scene." *Administration,* 14 (Autumn, 1966), 204-215.

Deutsch, Karl. "Social Mobilization and Political Development." *American Political Science Review,* 55 (September, 1961), 463-515.

Diamant, Alfred. "The Nature of Political Development." *Political Development and Social Change.* Jason L. Finkle and Richard W. Gable, eds. New York: John Wiley & Sons, 1966.

Eckstein, Harry. "Authority Relations and Governmental Performance: A Theoretical Framework." *Comparative Political Studies,* 2 (October, 1969), 269-325.

"Dublin, The Gun in Politics." *New Statesman,* October 30, 1954, p. 523.

Edwards, R. Dudley. "Church and State in Modern Ireland." *Ireland in the War Years and After, 1939-51.* Kevin B. Nolan and T. Desmond Williams, eds. Dublin: Gill and Macmillan, 1969.

Fallers, Lloyd. "Equality, Modernity, and Democracy in the New States." *Old Societies and New States: The Quest for Modernity in Asia and Africa.* Clifford Geertz, ed. New York: The Free Press of Glencoe, 1963.

Farrell, Brian. "Dáil Deputies: The 1969 Generation." *Economic and Social Review,* 2 (April, 1971), 309-27.

_____. "Labour and the Irish Political Party System: A Suggested Approach to Analysis," *Economic and Social Review,* vol. 1 (July, 1970), 477-502.

_____. "The New State and Irish Political Culture." *Administration,* 16 (Autumn, 1968), 238-46.

_____. "A Note on the Dáil Constitution, 1919." *The Irish Jurist,* 4 (Summer, 1969), 128-38.

Fennell, Desmond. "New Structures in the Church: Parish Councils." *Christus Rex,* 23 (October, November, December, 1969), 274-86.

"Fifth Annual Delegate Conference of the Irish Congress of Trade Unions." *International Labour Review,* 89 (March, 1964), 294-96.

"Gallup Poll," *Nusight* (October, 1969; December, 1969; April, 1970).

Geertz, Clifford. "The Integrative Revolution: Primordial Sentiments and Civil Politics in the New States." *Old Societies and New States: The Quest for Modernity in Asia and Africa.* Clifford Geertz, ed. New York: The Free Press of Glencoe, 1963.

"The Ginger Man." *Economist,* April 22, 1967, pp. 342-44.

Good, James. "The Role of the Priest in Education." *Christus Rex,* 23 (October, November, December, 1969), 287-92.

Gregor, A. James. "Political Science and the Uses of Functional Analysis." *American Political Science Review,* 62 (June, 1968), 425-39.

Greeley, Andrew W. and McCready, William C. "An Ethnic Group Which Vanished: The Strange Case of the American Irish." *Social Studies,* 1 (January, 1972), 38-50.

Guthrie, Tyrone. "Close-up of Ireland's Basic Problem." *New York Times Magazine,* January 19, 1964, pp. 22-28.

Hannan, Damian. "Kinship, Neighborhood and Social Change in Irish Rural Communities." *Economic and Social Review,* 3 (January, 1972), 163-88.

Hart, Ian. "Education and the Public Service: 2." *Leargas: A Review of Public Affairs,* June-July, 1967, pp. 7-11.

_____. "Public Opinion on Civil Servants and the Role and Power of the Individual in the Local Community." *Administration,* 18 (Winter, 1970), 375-91.

Heaney, Henry J. "Priest and Layman in Ireland: the Past." *Christus Rex,* 20 (July, August, September, 1966), 204-212.

Hogan, G. P. S. "The Constitutional Basis of Financial Controls." *Administration,* 7 (Summer, 1959), 155-65.

"Holidays With Pay." *International Labour Review,* 85 (June, 1962), 636-38.

Huntington, Samuel. "The Change to Change: Modernization, Development, and Politics." *Comparative Politics* 3 (April, 1971).

"Irish Censors Deny Entry to John McGahern Novel." *Publisher's Weekly,* October 11, 1965. p. 40.

Jones, Merwyn. "Unfinished Revolution: Prosperity in Sight, Freedom in Doubt." *New Statesman,* July 1, 1966, pp. 10-13.

Kaim-Caudle, P. R. "The Future of Social Services in the Irish Republic." *Administration,* 15 (Winter, 1967), 340-54.

Kane, Eileen. "Man and Kin in Donegal: A Study of Kinship Functions in a Rural Irish and an Irish-American Community," *Ethnology,* 7 (July, 1968), 245-58.

Keating, John. "The Slave Mind in Ireland." *The Voices of Ireland.* William G. Fitz-Gerald, ed. Manchester: John Heywood, [1924].

Kelleher, John V. "Ireland: And Where Does She Stand? " *Foreign Affairs,* 35 (April, 1957), 485-95.

Kelly, Gerard. "The Priest and the Layman in Ireland: The Present." *Christus Rex,* 20 (July, August, September, 1966), 212-17.

Kim, Young C. "The Concept of Political Culture in Comparative Politics." *Journal of Politics,* 26 (May, 1964), 313-36.

Lakeman, Enid. "A Sense of Proportion: The Irish General Election, 1965." *Contemporary Review,* 206 (May, 1965), 229-33.

Larkin, Emmet. "Socialism and Catholicism in Ireland." *Church History,* 33 (December, 1964), 462-83.

Lawless, Michael. "The Dáil Electoral System." *Administration,* 5 (Spring, 1957), 57-74.

Lee, Gerard A. "Fundamental Rights in the Irish Constitution." *Christus Rex,* 23 (April, May, June, 1969), 138-47.

Lemass, Sean T. "The Role of the State-Sponsored Bodies in the Economy." *Administration,* 6 (Winter, 1959), 277-95.

Leon, Donald E. "Advisory Bodies in Irish Central Government." *Administration,* 10 (Spring, 1962), 36-47.

Levy, Marion J., Jr. "Patterns (Structures) of Modernization and Political Development." *The Annals of the American Academy of Political and Social Science,* 358 (March, 1965), 29-40.

Linehan, Thomas P. "The Growth of the Civil Service." *Administration,* 2 (Summer, 1954), 61-73.

Livingston, William S. "A Note on the Nature of Federalism." *Political Science Quarterly,* 67 (March, 1952), 81-95.

Logue, Michael, Cardinal. "The Voice of the Church on Internal Strife." *The Voices of Ireland.* William Fitz-Gerald, ed. Manchester: John Heywood, [1924].

Lynch, Patrick. "The Economics of Independence: Some Unsettled Questions of Irish Economics." *Administration,* 7 (Summer, 1959), 91-108.

_____. "The Social Revolution that Never Was." *The Irish Struggle: 1916-1926.* Desmond Williams, ed. London: Routledge & Kegan Paul, 1966.

Mac Aonghusa, Proinsias. "Ecumenism in Dublin." *New Statesman,* February 11, 1966, p. 186.

_____. "Ireland's Divorce Battle." *New Statesman,* December 22, 1967, pp. 874-75.

McCarthy, Eoin. "Church and People in Ireland." *Christus Rex,* 16 (October, November, December 1963), 254-65.

McCartney, Charles. "Trade Unions and Economic Planning in Ireland." *International Labour Review,* 94 (July, 1966), 54-72.

McCartney, Donal. "Gaelic Ideological Origins of 1916." *1916: The Easter Rising.* O. Dudley Edwards and Fergus Pyle, eds. London: MacGibbon & Kee, 1968.

McHugh, Roger. "The Catholic Church and the Rising." *1916: The Easter Rising.* O. Dudley Edwards and Fergus Pyle, eds. London: MacGibbon & Kee, 1968.

McKenna, J.; Benevenuta, Sister; Brugha, R.; Cathcart, R.; McGillicuddy, T.; O'Donoghue, M.; Williams, T. D. "The Teaching of History in Irish Schools." *Administration,* 15 (Winter, 1967), 268-85.

Martin, Conor, "Attitudes to Political Life." *Administration,* 15 (Winter, 1967), 261-67.

Martindale, Don. "The Sociology of National Character." *The Annals of the American Academy of Political and Social Science,* 370 (March, 1967), 30-35.

Mathuna, S. O. "The Christian and the Civil Service." *Administration,* 3 69-74.

Meghen, J. "Social History." *The Limerick Rural Survey.* Jeremiah Newman, ed. Tipperary: Muintirnatir Rural Publications, 1964.

Meagher, G. A. "Housing and the Tax Payer." *Administration,* 2 (Winter, 1954-55), 56-66.

"Mr. DeValera's Failure: The End of an Era." *Round Table,* 49 (September, 1959), 361-64.

Murphy, John A. "The Irish Party System, 1938-51." *Ireland in the War Years and After, 1939-51.* Kevin Nolan and T. Desmond Williams, eds. Dublin: Gill and McMillan, 1969.

_____. "Priests and People in Modern Irish History." *Christus Rex,* 23 (October, November, December, 1969), 235-59.

Murray, C. H. "National and Physical Planning." *Administration,* 14 (Winter, 1966), 286-97.

_____. "Public Affairs, 1916-1966: The Economic Scene." *Administration,* 14 (Autumn, 1966), 199-203.

Nordlinger, Eric. "Political Development: Time Sequences and Rates of Change." *World Politics,* 20 (April, 1968), 494-520.

O'Connor. T. M. "Local Government and Community Development." *Administration,* 11 (Winter, 1963), 296-310.

O'Danachair, Caoimhin. "The Family in Irish Tradition." *Christus Rex,* 16 (July, August, September, 1962), 185-96.

O'Doherty, Thomas, Bishop. "Of Rulers and Citizens: Essay on Duties and Rights." *The Voices of Ireland.* William Fitz-Gerald, ed. Manchester: John Heywood [1924].

O'Hanlon, Roderick. "A Constitution for a Free People." *Administration,* 15 (Summer, 1967), 85-101.

O'Leary, Cornelius. "Administration in the Irish Republic." *Political Studies,* 14 (June, 1966), 223-25.

Pye, Lucian W. "The Concept of Political Development." *The Annals of the American Academy of Political and Social Science,* 358 (March, 1965), 1-13.

Pyne, Peter. "The Third Sinn Fein Party: 1923-1926." *Eire-Ireland* 1 (October, 1969), 29-50, and (January, 1970), 230-257.

Raifeartaigh, T. O. "The States' Administration of Education." *Administration,* 2 (Winter, 1954-55), 67-77.

Roche, Desmond. "Local Government Reorganization: The Issue Involved." *Administration,* 19 (Winter, 1971), 318-327.

Rustow, Dankwart A. "New Horizons for Comparative Politics." *World Politics,* 9 (July, 1957), 530-49.

Sacks, Paul M. "Balliwicks, Locality, and Religion: Three Elements in an Irish Dáil Constituency Election." *Economic and Social Review,* 1 (July, 1970), 531-554.

Schmitt, David E. "Aspects of Irish Social Organization and Administrative Development," *Administration* 18 (Winter, 1970), 392-404.

Scully, Michael. "Oireachtas Control of Public Corporations." *Administration,* 2 (Spring, 1954), 33-42.

Searing, Donald D. "The Comparative Study of Elite Socialization." *Comparative Political Studies,* 1 (January, 1969), 471-500.

Smyth, John M. "Seanad Eireann–1." *Administration,* 15 (Winter, 1967), 301-307.

"Sons and Widows." *Economist,* March 20, 1965, p. 1259.

"Taxing the Irish Way." *Economist,* April 2, 1966, pp. 66-67.

Thornley, David A. "Ireland, The End of an Era." *Studies,* 58 (1964), 1-17.
_____. "Television and Politics." *Administration,* 15 (Autumn, 1967), 217-25.

"Towards Labour Unity." *New Statesman,* January 21, 1956, p. 59.

Troy, T. "Some Aspects of Parliamentary Questions." *Administration,* 7 (Autumn, 1959), 251-59.

"The Turnover Tax." *New Statesman,* November 8, 1963, pp. 640-41.

Viney, Ethna. "Women in Rural Ireland." *Christus Rex,* 22 (October, November, December, 1968), 333-42.

Viney, Michael. "Growing Old in Ireland." Dublin: *The Irish Times,* n.d.

Ward, Robert, "Political Modernization and Political Culture in Japan." *World Politics,* 15 (July, 1963), 569-96.

"What Chances for a Bright Poor Child." *Economist,* December 10, 1966, p. 1124.

Whitaker, T. K. "Economic Planning in Ireland." *Administration,* 14 (Winter, 1966), 277-85.

Williams, Edward J. "Latin American Catholicism and Political Integration." *Comparative Political Studies,* 2 (October, 1969), 342-49.

Wilson, James Q. "Generational and Ethnic Differences Among Career Police Officers," *American Journal of Sociology,* 59 (March, 1964) 522-28.

Wilson, Desmond. "The Priest and the Community." *Christus Rex,* 20 (January, February, March, 1966), 38-47.

Woodhouse, H. F. "University Merger Problematic." *Christian Century,* August 7, 1968, pp. 1000-1002.

Books, Monographs, and Unpublished Papers

Adams, Michael. *Censorship: The Irish Experience.* Dublin: Scepter Books, 1968.

Adorno. T. W., *et al. The Authoritarian Personality.* New York: Harper & Row, 1950.

Akenson, Donald. *The Irish Education Experiment: The National System of Education in the Nineteenth Century.* London: Routledge & Kegan Paul, 1970. Toronto: University of Toronto Press, 1970.

Almond, Gabriel A., and Coleman, James S., eds. *The Politics of the Developing Areas.* Princeton, N. J.: Princeton University Press, 1960.

_____, and Powell, G. Bingham. *Comparative Politics: A Developmental Approach.* Boston: Little, Brown, 1966.

_____, and Verba, Sidney. *The Civic Culture: Political Attitudes and Democracy in Five Nations.* Boston: Little, Brown, 1963.

Arensberg, Conrad M. *The Irish Countryman: An Anthropological Study.* London: Macmillan, 1937.

_____, and Kimball, Solon T. *Family and Community in Ireland.* Cambridge, Mass.: Harvard University Press, 1940.

Arthur, George. *General Sir John Maxwell.* London: Murray, 1932.

Atkinson, Norman. *Irish Education: A History of Educational Institutions.* Dublin: Allen Figgis, 1969.

Bagenal, Philip H. *The American Irish and their Influence on Irish Politics.* London: K. Paul, Trench, 1882.

Banfield, Edward C. *The Moral Basis of a Backward Society.* Glencoe, Ill.: The Free Press, 1958.

Barker, Ernest. *National Character and the Factors in Its Formation.* 4th ed. rev. London: Methuen & Co., 1948.

Bartholomew, Paul C. *The Irish Judiciary.* Dublin: Institute of Public Administration, 1971.

Beasley, Pierce. *Michael Collins and the Making of New Ireland.* New York: Harper, 1926.

Beckett, C. J. *The Making of Modern Ireland 1603-1923.* London: Faber and Faber, 1966.

_____. *A Short History of Ireland.* London: Hutchinson's University Library, 1951.

Bence-Jones, Mark. *The Remarkable Irish. Chronicle of a Land, a Culture, a Mystique.* New York: McKay Co., 1966.

Beth, Loren. *The Development of Judicial Review in Ireland, 1937-1966.* Dublin: Institute of Public Administration, 1967.

Binder, Leonard et al. *Crises and Sequences in Political Development.* Princeton: Princeton University Press, 1971.

Birmingham, George A. *Irishmen All.* London: T. N. Foulis, 1913.

Blanchard, Jean. *The Church in Contemporary Ireland.* Dublin: Clonmore & Reynolds, 1963.

Boyd, Andrew. *Holy War in Belfast: A History of the Troubles in Northern Ireland.* New York: Grove Press, 1969.

Bristow, J. A., and Tait, A. A., eds. *Economic Policy in Ireland.* Dublin: Institute of Public Administration, 1968.

Brody, Hugh *Innishkillane: Change and Decline in the West of Ireland.* London: Allen Lane, The Penguin Press, 1973.

Bromage, Mary C. *De Valera and the March of a Nation.* New York: Noonday Press, 1957.

Budge, Ian, and O'Leary, Cornelius. *Belfast: Approach to Crisis, A Study of Belfast Politics 1613-1970.* London: Macmillan, 1973.

Chauvire, Roger. *A Short History of Ireland.* New York: New American Library, 1965.

Chesterton, Gilbert K. *Irish Impressions.* London: W. Collins & Sons, 1919.

Chubb, Basil. *The Government: An Introduction to the Cabinet System in Ireland.* Dublin: Institute of Public Administration, 1961.

_____. *The Government and Politics of Ireland.* Stanford: Stanford University Press, 1970. London: Oxford University Press, 1970.

Chubb, Basil and Lynch, Patrick, eds. *Economic Development and Planning.* Dublin: Institute of Public Administration, 1969.

Clarkson, J. Dunsmore. *Labour and Nationalism in Ireland.* New York: Longmans, 1925.

Cohan, A. S. *The Irish Political Elite.* Dublin: Gill and MacMillan, 1972.

Coleman, James S., ed. *Education and Political Development.* Princeton, N. J.: Princeton University Press, 1965.

Collins, John. *Local Government.* Dublin: Institute of Public Administration, 1963.

Colum, Padraic. *The Road Round Ireland.* New York: The Macmillan Company, 1926.

Connery, Donald S. *The Irish.* New York: Simon and Schuster, 1968.

Connolly, James. *Labour in Ireland, Labour in Irish History, The Reconquest of Ireland.* Dublin: Maunsel & Co., 1917.

Coogan, Patrick. *Ireland Since the Rising.* New York: Frederick A. Praeger, 1966.

Crosland, T. W. H. *The Wild Irishman.* London: T. Werner Laurie, 1905.

Crozier, Michael. *The Bureaucratic Phenomenon.* Chicago: University of Chicago Press, 1964.

Cullen, Kathleen. *School and Family: Social Factors in Educational Attainment.* Dublin: Gill and Macmillan, 1969.

Cullen, L. M. *Life in Ireland.* New York: G. P. Putnam's Sons, 1968.

Curtayne, Alice. *The Irish Story: A Survey of Irish History and Culture.* New York: Kenedy, 1960.

Curtis, Edmund. *A History of Ireland.* 6th ed. New York: Barnes & Noble, 1961.

Curtis, Lewis P. *Coercion and Conciliation in Ireland, 1880-92: A Study in Conservative Unionism.* Princeton, N. J.: Princeton University Press, 1963.

Dawson, Richard E., and Prewitt, Kenneth. *Political Socialization.* Boston: Little, Brown, 1969.

DePaor, Liam. *Divided Ulster.* 2nd ed. Middlesex, England: Penguin Books, 1972.

Dillon, Myles, ed. *Early Irish Society.* Dublin: Colm O Lochlainn for the Cultural Relations Committee of Ireland, 1954.

Donaldson, Loraine. *Development Planning in Ireland.* New York: Praeger, 1965.

Duverger, Maurice. *Political Parties: Their Organization and Activities in the Modern State.* Translated by Barbara and Robert North, New York: Wiley, 1954.

Dye, Thomas R., and Zeigler, Harmon L. *The Irony of Democracy: An Uncommon Introduction to American Politics.* Belmont, California: Wadsworth, 1970.

Eckstein, Harry. *Division and Cohesion in Democracy: A Study of Norway.* Princeton: Princeton University Press, 1966.

Edwards, O. Dudley, and Pyle, Fergus, eds. *1916: The Easter Rising.* London: MacGibbon & Kee, 1968.

Enloe, Cynthia. *Ethnic Conflict and Political Development.* Boston: Little, Brown, 1973.

Evans, Emyr E. *Irish Folk Ways,* London: Routledge & Kegan Paul, 1957.

Farley, Desmond. *Social Insurance and Social Assistance in Ireland.* Dublin: Institute of Public Administration, 1964.

Farrell, Brian. *Chairman or Chief: The Role of the Taoiseach in Irish Government.* Dublin: Gill and Macmillan, 1971.

_____. *The Founding of Dáil Eireann: Parliament and Nation Building.* Dublin: Gill and Macmillan, 1971.

Finkle, Jason L., and Gable, Richard W. *Political Development and Social Change.* New York: John Wiley, 1966.

Finlay, Ian. *The Civil Service.* Dublin: Institute of Public Administration, 1966.

FitzGerald, Garret. *State-Sponsored Bodies.* 2nd. ed. rev. Dublin: Institute of Public Administration, 1963.

Garvin, Thomas. *The Irish Senate.* Dublin: Institute of Public Administration, 1969.

Gray, Tony. *The Irish Answer.* Boston: Little, Brown, 1966.

Geertz, Clifford, ed. *Old Societies and New States: The Quest for Modernity in Asia and Africa.* New York: The Free Press of Glencoe, 1963.

Green, Alice Stopford. *Irish Nationality.* rev. ed. London: Williams & Northgate, 1911.

Gwynn, Denis. *The Irish Free State, 1922-1927.* London: Macmillan and Co., 1928.

Gwynn, Stephan. *Ireland.* London: Ernest Benn, 1924.

Hackett, Francis. *Ireland: A Study in Nationalism.* New York: B. W. Huebsch, 1918.

Harris, Rosemary. *Prejudice and Tolerance in Ulster: A Study of Neighbors and 'Strangers' in a Border Community.* Manchester: Manchester University Press, 1972.

Hayden, Mary and Moonan, George A. *A Short History of the Irish People, pt. 2, From 1603 to Modern Times.* rev. ed. Dublin: Educational Company of Ireland, 1960.

Healy, Timothy Michael. *Letters and Leaders of My Day.* London: Butterworth, 1928.

Heslinga, M. W. *The Irish Border as a Cultural Divide.* Assen, The Netherlands: Van Gorcum, 1971.

Holt, Edgar. *Protest in Arms: The Irish Troubles, 1916-23.* New York: Coward-McCann, 1961.

Hughes, Katherine. *English Atrocities in Ireland: A Compilation of Facts from Court and Press Records.* New York: Friends for Irish Freedom Inc., 1920.

Hull, Elenor. *A History of Ireland and Her People.* London: Harrap, 1931.

Humphreys, Alexander J. *New Dubliners.* London: Routledge & Kegan Paul, 1966.

Huntington, Samuel. *Political Order in Changing Societies.* New Haven: Yale University Press, 1968.

Hurley, Michael. S. J. *Irish Anglicanism: 1869-1969.* Dublin: Allen Figgis, 1970.

Hutchinson, Bertram. *Social Status and Inter-Generational Social Mobility in Dublin.* Dublin: Economic and Social Research Institute, 1969.

Inglis, Brian. *The Story of Ireland.* London: Faber and Faber, 1956.

Jennings, Ivor. *The Queen's Government.* rev. ed. Middlesex, England: Penguin Books, 1965.

Johnston, Harry H. *Views and Reviews from the Outlook of an Anthropologist.* London: Williams & Norgate, 1912.

Joyce, James. *A Portrait of the Artist as a Young Man.* New York: The Viking Press, 1961.

Kaim-Caudle, P. R. *Social Policy in the Irish Republic.* London: Routledge and Kegan Paul, 1967.

Kaufman, Robert R. *The Patron-Client Concept and Macro-Politics: Prospects and Problems.* Paper prepared for delivery at the 1972 Annual Meeting of the American Political Science Association, Washington, D. C., September 4-9, 1972.

Kelly, Henry. *How Storment Fell.* Dublin: Gill and Macmillan, 1972.

Kohn, Leo. *The Constitution of the Irish Free State.* London: George Allen & Unwin, 1932.

Lecky, William E. H. *Leaders of Public Opinion in Ireland.* New York: Longmans, Green, & Co., 1903.

Leon, Donald E. *Advisory Bodies in Irish Government.* Dublin: Institute of Public Affairs, 1963.

Lockington, W. J. *The Soul of Ireland.* New York: Macmillan, 1920.

Lucey, Denis I. F., and Kaldor, Donald R. *Rural Industrialization: The Impact of Industrialization on Two Rural Communities in Western Ireland.* Dublin: Chapman, 1969.

Lynd, Robert. *Home Life in Ireland.* London: Mills & Boon, 1909.

_____. *Ireland a Nation.* London: Grant Richards, 1919.

Lynn, Richard. *The Irish Brain Drain.* Dublin: The Economic and Social Research Institute, 1968.

Lyons, F. S. L. *Ireland Since the Famine.* New York: Charles Scribner's Sons, 1971.

_____. *The Irish Parliamentary Party: 1890-1910.* London: Faber and Faber, 1951.

Macardle, Dorothy. *The Irish Republic: A Documented Chronicle of the Anglo-Irish Conflict and the Partitioning of Ireland, With a Detailed Account of the Period, 1916-1923.* New York: Farrer, Straus, and Giroux, 1965.

McCarthy, Charles. *The Distasteful Challenge.* Dublin: Institute of Public Administration, 1968.

McCarthy, Michael J. F. *Irish Land and Irish Liberty: A Study of the New Lords of the Soil.* London: R. Scott, 1911.

McCracken, J. L. *Representative Government in Ireland: A Study of Dáil Eireann: 1919-48.* London: Oxford University Press, 1958.

McDowell, R. B. *The Irish Administration, 1801-1914.* Toronto: University of Toronto Press, 1964.

_____. *Public Opinion and Government Policy in Ireland, 1801-1846.* London: Faber and Faber, 1952.

McDunphy, Michael. *The President of Ireland: His Powers, Functions, and Duties.* Dublin: Browne and Nolan, 1945.

McElligott, T. J. *Education in Ireland.* Dublin: Institute of Public Administration, 1966.

MacManus, Francis, ed. *The Years of the Great Test: 1926-39.* Cork: Mercier Press, 1967.

McNamara, Brinsley. *The Valley of the Squinting Windows.* Dublin: Maunsel, 1918.

MacNaill, Eoin. *Phases of Irish History.* Dublin: M. H. Gill & Son, 1919.

Manning, Maurice. *The Blueshirts.* Toronto: University of Toronto Press, 1971.

_____. *Irish Political Parties: An Introduction.* Dublin: Gill and Macmillan, 1972.

Mansergh, Nicholas. *Ireland in the Age of Reform and Revolution: A Commentary on Anglo-Irish Relations and on Political Forces in Ireland, 1840-1921.* London: George Allen & Unwin, 1940.

_____. *The Irish Free State: Its Government and Politics.* London: George Allen & Unwin, 1934.

Martin, F. X., ed. *Leaders and Men of the Easter Rising: Dublin 1916.* London: Methuen & Co., 1967.

Moody, Theodore William, and Martin, F. X., eds. *The Course of Irish History.* New York: Weybright and Tulley, 1967.

Moss, Warner. *Political Parties in the Irish Free State.* New York: Columbia University Press, 1933.

Muimhneachain, M. O. *The Functions of the Department of the Taoiseach.* Dublin: Institute of Public Administration, 1960.

Munger, Frank. *The Legitimacy of Opposition: The Change of Government in Ireland in 1932.* Paper prepared for delivery at the 1966 Annual Meeting of the American Political Science Association, New York City, September 6-10, 1966.

Neeson, Eoin. *The Civil War in Ireland.* Cork: Mercier Press, 1966.

Newman, Jeremiah, ed. *The Limerick Rural Survey: 1958-1964.* Tipperary: Muintir na Tire Rural Publications, 1964.

Nowlan, Kevin B. and Williams, T. Desmond, eds. *Ireland in the War Years and After, 1939-51.* Dublin: Gill and Macmillan, 1969.

Norman, E. R. *The Catholic Church and Ireland in the Age of Rebellion, 1859-1873.* London: Longmans Green & Co., 1965.

O'Brien, Conor Cruise. *States of Ireland.* London: Hutchinson & Co., 1972.

O'Callaghan, Sean. *The Easter Lily: The Story of the I. R. A.* London: Allan Wingate, 1956.

O'Cinneide, Seamus. *A Law for the Poor: A Study of Home Assistance in Ireland.* Dublin: Institute of Public Administration, 1970.

O'Corcora, Donall. *What's This About the Gaelic League?* Dublin: Gaelic League, 1942.

O'Donnell, James D. *How Ireland Is Governed.* Dublin: Institute of Public Administration, 1967.

O'Faolain, Sean. *The Irish: A Character Study.* New York: Devin-Adair Co., 1956.

O'Mahony, Charles. *The Viceroys of Ireland.* London: J. Long, 1912.

O'Mahony, David. *Industrial Relations in Ireland: The Background.* Dublin: Economic and Social Research Institute, 1964.

O'Riordan, Michael. *Catholocity and Progress in Ireland.* London: K. Paul, Trench, Trubner & Co., 1906. St. Louis: B. Herder, 1906.

O'Sullivan, Donal Joseph. *The Irish Free State and Its Senate: A Study in Contemporary Politics.* London: Faber and Faber, 1940.

Parsons, Talcott, and Shils, Edward, eds. *Toward A General Theory of Action.* Cambridge, Mass.: Harvard University Press, 1951.

Paul-Dubois, L. *Contemporary Ireland.* Dublin: Maunsel & Co., 1908.

_____. *The Irish Struggle and Its Results.* Translated by T. P. Gill. London: Longmans, Green & Co., 1934.

Pearse, Padraic H. *Political Writings and Speeches.* Dublin: The Talbot Press, 1952.

Penthony, P. *Psychological Barriers to Economic Achievement.* Dublin: Economic and Social Research Institute, 1965.

Pinney, Edward L., ed. *Comparative Politics and Political Theory.* Chapel Hill: University of North Carolina Press, 1966.

Plunkett, Horace. *Ireland in the New Century.* London: John Murray, 1904.

Pocock, G. J. A. *The Case of Ireland Truly Stated: Revolutionary Politics in the Context of Increasing Stabilization.* Washington University, Department of History (Unpublished paper), 1966.

Pye, Lucian W. *Politics, Personality, and Nation-Building: Burma's Search for Identity.* New Haven: Yale University Press, 1962.

_____, and Verba, Sidney, eds. *Political Culture and Political Development.* Princeton, N. J.: Princeton University Press, 1965.

Redford, Emmette S. *Democracy in the Administrative State.* London and New York: Oxford University Press, 1969.

Riggs, Fred. *Thailand: The Modernizaton of a Bureaucratic Polity.* Honolulu: East-West Center Press, 1966.

Rose, Richard. *Governing Without Consensus: An Irish Perspective.* Boston: Beacon Press, 1971.

Ross, J. F. S. *The Irish Election System: What It Is and How It Works.* London: Pall Mall Press, 1959.

Rumpf, E. *Nationalismus und Sozialismus in Irland.* Meisenheim am Glan, 1959.

Russell, George W. *The National Being: Some Thoughts on an Irish Polity.* Dublin: Maunsel & Co., 1916.

Scott, James C. *Comparative Political Corruption.* Englewood Cliffs, N. J.: Prentice-Hall, 1972.

Shaw, G. Bernard. *How to Settle the Irish Question.* Dublin: Talbot Press, 1917.

_____. *The Matter with Ireland.* New York: Hill & Wang, 1962.

Sheehy, Michael. *Divided We Stand: A Study of Partition.* New York: Putnam, 1956.

Smith, Donald E. *Religion and Political Development.* Boston: Little, Brown, 1970.

Smith, John McG. *The Theory and Practice of the Irish Senate.* Dublin: Institute of Public Administration, 1972.

Smith-Gordon, Lionel, and Staples, Lawrence C. *Rural Reconstruction in Ireland: A Record of Co-operative Organization.* London: P. S. King & Sons, 1917.

Smyth, J. C. *The Houses of Oireachtas.* 2nd ed. rev. Dublin: Institute of Public Administration, 1964.

Somerville, Edith A. O. and Ross, Martin. *The Smile and the Tear.* 2nd ed. London: Methuen, 1933.

Stewart, A. T. Q. *The Ulster Crisis.* London: Faber and Faber, 1967.

Strauss, Eric. *Irish Nationalism and British Democracy.* New York: Columbia University Press, 1951.

Sunday Times Insight Team. *Ulster.* Baltimore: Penguin, 1972.

Tracy, Honor. *Mind You, I've Said Nothing!: Forays in the Irish Republic.* London: Methuen & Co., 1953.

Trench, W. Stewart. *Realities of Irish Life.* London: Longmans, Green and Co., 1869.

Ussher, Arland. *The Face and Mind of Ireland.* London: Gollancz, 1949.

Ward, Alan J. *Cabinet Government and Political Power in the Irish Republic.* Paper prepared for delivery at the 1973 Annual Conference of the American Committee for Irish Studies, Ann Arbor, Michigan, May 3-5, 1973.

Ward, Robert E. *Studying Politics Abroad: Field Research in The Developing Areas.* Boston: Little, Brown, 1964.

_____, and Rustow, Dankwart A., eds. *Political Modernization in Japan and Turkey.* Princeton, N. J.: Princeton University Press, 1964.

Weber, Max. *The Protestant Ethic and the Spirit of Capitalism.* Translated by Talcott Parsons. New York: Charles Scribner's Sons, 1958.

Wells, Warre B. *Irish Indiscretions.* Dublin: Maunsel and Roberts, 1923.

White, Terence de Vere. *Ireland.* London: Thames and Hudson, 1968.

_____. *Kevin O'Higgins.* Tralee: Anvil Books, 1966.

Whyte, John H. *Dáil Deputies: Their Work, Its Difficulties, Possible Remedies.* Dublin: Tuairim Society, 1966.

_____. *Church and State in Modern Ireland, 1923-1970.* Dublin: Gill and Macmillan, 1971.

Williams, Desmond, ed. *The Irish Struggle, 1916-1926.* London: Routledge & Kegan Paul, 1966.

Woods, Michael. *Research in Ireland: Key to Economic and Social Development.* Dublin: Institute of Public Administration, 1969.

Wylie, Laurence. *Village in the Vaucluse.* Cambridge, Mass.: Harvard University Press, 1957.

Younger, Calton. *A State of Disunion.* London: Frederick Muller, 1972.

Index

Index

About the Author

David E. Schmitt received the B. A. degree in 1961 from Miami University (Ohio) where he majored in government. After four years of service as an officer in the U. S. Navy, he began graduate studies at The University of Texas at Austin, completing the Ph. D. in government in 1971. Dr. Schmitt and his wife, formerly Gabrielle Condron of Charleville, County Cork, Ireland, have two children. Irish politics, comparative government, and public administration constitute Dr. Schmitt's main research and publishing interests. Since September, 1970 Professor Schmitt has taught political science at Northeastern University in Boston, Massachusetts.

J6